MW01618128

The Art of Being Unseen

Letterpress Works by Sandy Tilcock 1986–2013

Compilation by Dennis Hyatt and Sandy Tilcock

Luminare Press ❖ Eugene, Oregon

The Art of Being Unseen

Last stanza in "Famous" from *Words Under the Words: Selected Poems*, The Eighth Mountain Press, A Far Corner Book, Portland, Oregon, © 1995 by Naomi Shihab Nye. Used with permission of the author.

Printed in the United States of America

Cover Design: Sandy Tilcock and Dune Erickson

Luminare Press
467 W 17th Ave
Eugene, OR 97401
www.luminarepress.com

LCCN: 2014946568
ISBN: 978-1-937303-33-4

I want to be famous in the way a pulley is famous,
or a buttonhole, not because it did anything spectacular,
but because it never forgot what it could do.

—NAOMI SHIHAB NYE

CONTENTS

INTRODUCTORY NOTE

The ninety-eight works listed in this book were designed and printed by Sandy Tilcock. The list includes commission work by Sandy. Omitted are binding commissions and any job printing.

As a teacher, mentor, collaborator, and supporter of the printing arts, Sandy has provided printing and design skills, instruction, technical and artistic advice, and studio resources for the benefit of many other artists and their works, which are acknowledged in their colophons. She has furthermore created unique bindings and boxes, first as a student in the MFA program at the University of Alabama and later as commissions, for the printing and art projects designed by others.

Thus, many works associated with Sandy Tilcock and her lone goose press are outside the intended scope of the entries selected for listing and description in this book. A diligent search of exhibition catalogs, the holdings of library special collections, the lone goose press archives, the Knight Library Press archives, and news articles will reveal the broad extent of her influence and work in fine press publications created by others.

— DENNIS HYATT

“It is not about me, but about letting the work of writers and artists shine through the craft.”

Go back to the late 50s, early 60s in the small farming community of Nampa, Idaho, twenty-five miles or so from Boise. I loved to read but I only had access to books through the library. Once or twice a year my parents and I would travel to Boise to shop. It was a big deal then, an all-day trip. My father liked to spend time in a camera shop, which was next door to a used bookstore. My parents discovered they could leave me in the bookstore for several hours while they ran errands. I would wander the aisles and contemplate the books with complete fascination—admonished by my parents to never touch. When they retrieved me, the store proprietors would compliment my exemplary behavior and I would be calm and content.

Fast forward to age fifteen. My mother asks me what I would like as a gift. A book, I tell her, hardcover—Hemingway’s *The Old Man and the Sea*. We go down to the stationery store, order the book and wait more than six weeks for delivery. I am ecstatic—my first hardcover book! I am as fascinated by its weight and feel as by its content. My mother thought three and a half dollars was pricey, but she indulged me. I still have the book. Aside from a tattered dust jacket, it is in pristine condition.

Now I am twenty-three, a graduate student in mathematics at Oregon State University, newly married and interested in photography. With the support of my husband I acquire a camera and set up a darkroom, and we are soon bestowing handmade cards on our friends using my photos. One friend suggests I take up calligraphy as a way to combine words with images. I find some excellent calligraphy teachers and soon gain a new enchantment with letterforms. In the course of my calligraphy studies, a one-day workshop to learn how to bind a personal journal starts me on my path to the world of making books. I continue my studies in lettering arts while pursuing the craft of bookbinding, reading and teaching myself. At a two-week lettering workshop on the coast in the late 70s, the instructor notices my journal. She asks who made it. I tell her, and she tells me to give up lettering and pursue the craft of bookbinding—I will excel at it, while I will be mediocre as a lettering artist. It was a hard message to hear, but I listened and turned my attention increasingly to bookbinding.

It is 1985. I am thirty-seven, a graduate student in the Book Arts Institute at the University of Alabama. One of my first letterpress projects is an excerpt, “March: The Geese Return” from a book I have long treasured, Aldo Leopold's *A Sand County Almanac*. In 1987 I enter into my first collaborative book project, *Acknowledging the Presence of the Other*, with my dear friend Rosi Gross-Smith. My passion for setting ink on paper and for the design and binding of books is kindled with these projects. Upon my return to Eugene, Oregon, I launch my own press, beginning what would be in many ways a solitary journey.

My work continues. It is not about me, but about letting the work of writers and artists shine through the craft I bring to the publications. My goal is to be like the buttonhole in Naomi Shihab Nye's poem that "… never forgot what it could do."

— SANDY TILCOCK

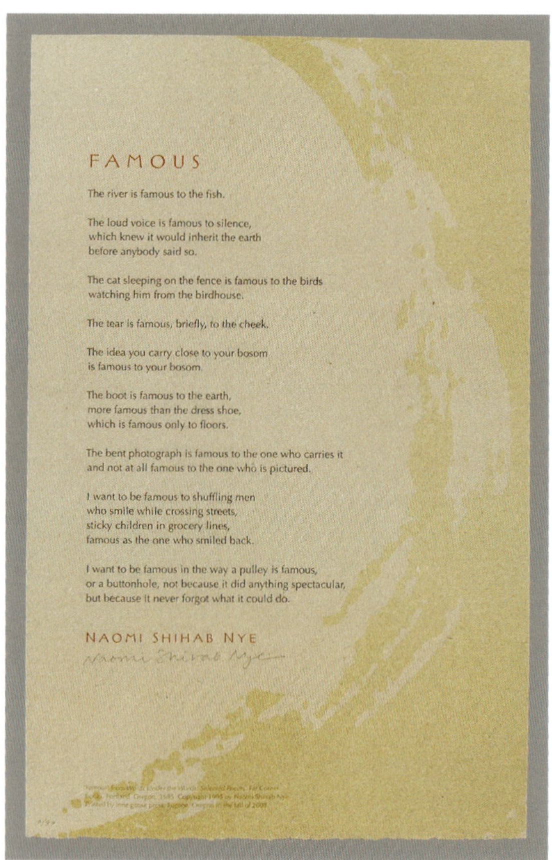

FAMOUS

The river is famous to the fish.

The loud voice is famous to silence,
which knew it would inherit the earth
before anybody said so.

The cat sleeping on the fence is famous to the birds
watching him from the birdhouse.

The tear is famous, briefly, to the cheek.

The idea you carry close to your bosom
is famous to your bosom.

The boot is famous to the earth,
more famous than the dress shoe,
which is famous only to floors.

The bent photograph is famous to the one who carries it
and not at all famous to the one who is pictured.

I want to be famous to shuffling men
who smile while crossing streets,
sticky children in grocery lines,
famous as the one who smiled back.

I want to be famous in the way a pulley is famous,
or a buttonhole, not because it did anything spectacular,
but because it never forgot what it could do.

NAOMI SHIHAB NYE

LGP22

Student Works 1986–1987

These projects were done while I was pursuing my degree at the University of Alabama. The director of the program, Gabriel Rummonds, required us to treat each assignment as if we were an established press. As part of this requirement, we each had to select a name for our press. As I was describing some of the culture-shock experiences of moving from Eugene to Tuscaloosa, a friend remarked, "You're lost in Loosa Land!" Hence Loosa Land Press.

STU1 **Flutterbys** **(1986)**

Haiku by Kyoshi and Wafu
Stencil images by Sandy Tilcock

4.3 x 5.5 inches, 4 pages

20 unnumbered copies

Handset Van Dijck type with titling in handset Cochin Open

Mulberry paper

Printed on a Vandercook SP-15 proof press

French fold pamphlet binding

Cover paper decorated using a stencil brush to form a stipple pattern that resembles the stippling of the interior stencils

Loosa Land Press

STU2 **Three Friends** **(1986)**

Kurt Brown, Gerard McGorian, and John Wentworth

9 x 6.1 inches, 16 pages

25 unnumbered copies

Handset Baskerville types

Mohawk Letterpress paper

Printed on a Vandercook SP-20 proof press

Pamphlet stitch in a paper wrapper

Wrapper paper with a printed collagraph by Sandy Tilcock

Loosa Land Press

This chapbook is the result of a friendship that developed with my neighbor, John Wentworth, in my first year at Alabama. John and the other two authors were poetry students in the Creative Writing Program.

STU3 **Do Not Burn Yourselves Out (1986)**

Edward Abbey
Collagraph by Sandy Tilcock

8.4 x 12.5 inches, single sheet broadside

20 unnumbered copies

Handset Perpetua types

Nideggen paper

Printed on a Vandercook SP-20 proof press

Presented in a paper wrapper bound in boards with red Iris bookcloth

Text for the broadside taken from a speech Edward Abbey made to environmentalists in Missoula, Montana in 1978

Loosa Land Press

STU4 **The Etiquette of Books (1986)**

Rabbi Judah ben Samuel Sir Leon Chassid

8.1 x 4.8 inches, 6 pages

20 unnumbered copies

Handset Bulmer types

Mohawk Superfine paper with Fabriano Ingres wrappers

Printed on a Vandercook SP-15 proof press

Accordion fold with first fold sewn into the paper wrapper

Text adapted from a translation of a portion of *Sefer Hasidim (The Book of the Pious)*, written circa 1190

Loosa Land Press

STU5 **An Excerpt from *A Sand County Almanac* (1987)**

Aldo Leopold
Geese silhouettes by Sandy Tilcock
Image on page 6

9 x 8.6 inches, 20 pages

25 numbered copies

Title calligraphy by Edie Roberts

Handset Spectrum types

Illustration and title lettering printed using magnesium plates

Tan Amora paper

Printed on a Vandercook SP-20 proof press

Sewn binding with a supported paper wrapper made from ruggine Fabriano Ingres paper

Excerpt from *A Sand County Almanac and Sketches Here and There*, Aldo Leopold (Oxford University Press, 1949)

Loosa Land Press

This was my first book. The assignment was to design, print, and bind a previously published text. We were to write and request permission from the publishers and send a copy to the publisher when done. I also sent a copy of the book to Leopold's son, Luna Leopold. Luna responded with a touching letter.

A Sand County Almanac had long been a favorite book. I was (and continue to be) very concerned about environmental issues. I was also enchanted by Canada Geese, who mark the passing seasons by their honking as they pass over on their winter/spring migrations. I chose to print the chapter "March: The Geese Return" and it is from this chapter that I would eventually determine the name for my press.

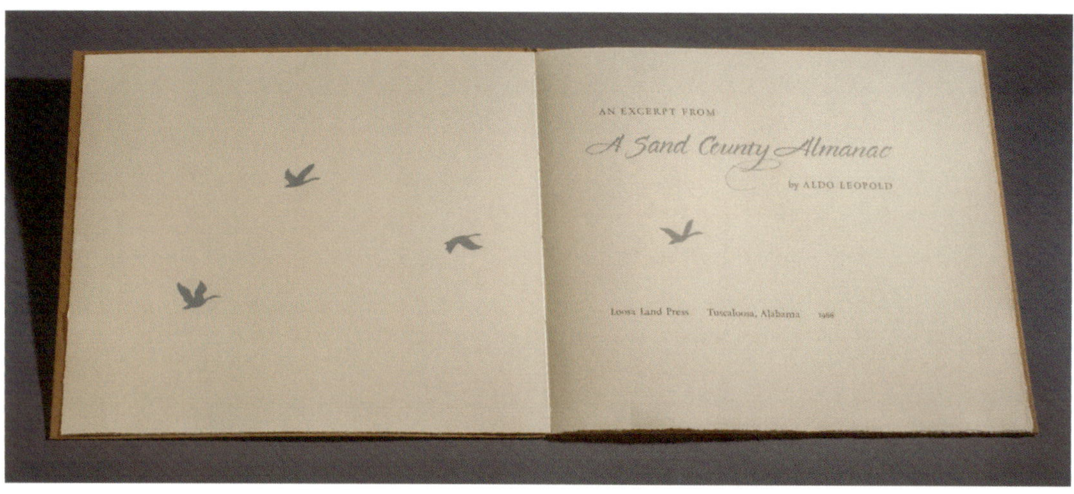

STU5

STU6 **Elevation Toccata (1987)**

Patrick Tilcock

8.3 x 5.9 inches, 4 pages

25 unnumbered copies

Handset Baskerville types with titling in handset Cochin Open

Lana Laid paper

Printed on a Vandercook SP-20 proof press

French fold pamphlet binding

Paste paper cover by Sandy Tilcock and Rosalinda Gross-Smith

Loosa Land Press

My husband Patrick continued to live in Oregon while I was at Alabama. During that time he began writing poetry and sent me this poem prior to his visit in the spring of 1987 and the celebration of his 41st birthday. This keepsake was his birthday gift.

STU7 **Acknowledging the Presence of the Other (1987)**

Carolyn Servid
Illustration by Danielle Rougeau

6.7 x 12 inches, 20 pages

50 numbered copies signed by the author and the illustrator

Title calligraphy by Edie Roberts

Handset Van Dijck types

Illustration and title calligraphy printed using magnesium plates

Taupe Amora paper

Printed on a Vandercook 219 proof press

Bound in boards in quarter leather with paste paper over boards; a thin hand-torn tea chest silver paper band separates the join between the leather and paste paper

Paste paper by Sandy Tilcock and Rosalinda Gross-Smith

Labrador Press

This book was a collaborative endeavor with my closest friend in school, Rosalinda (Rosi) Gross-Smith. As binding majors, we asked the director of the program, Gabriel Rummonds, if there was an edition of books we could bind in order to gain experience in edition binding. His reply was "No. You need to design and print a book in order to do that." This is what we did, forming Labrador Press to honor the fact that we both owned Labrador dogs, Jennifer and Hyder-Sue. We solicited an original manuscript from a writer friend of Rosi's and set off on our adventure of publishing.

"The physical presence of books has its own divine mystery..."

Sandy and I are a mismatched couple if ever there was one. She is organized and dynamic; I am reflective, dreamy, and to put it kindly, somewhat casual in my habits. She was brought up on *Field and Stream*; I perused *The Diapason*, a journal for organists. I could go on, but being a lifelong contemplator, I want to contemplate the mystery of what brought us together and what has kept us engaged over these decades that today seem amazingly short, and to put this mystery in the context of Sandy's book arts work.

There are no definitive explanations, but there are markers that hint at the question. The first of these: dogs. It was Sandy who insisted that our life together include dogs. I did not require much persuading, and as a result we have been blessed, sometimes challenged and always enriched by a running total of eight canines over the forty-odd years we have been together. Our first two puppies witnessed Sandy's early exploration of photography. Her first enlarger was a homemade box we attached to an old bellows camera, and if I remember correctly, powered by a forty-watt appliance bulb. The darkroom consisted of waiting for a moonless night and drawing all the drapes. The puppies, Granger and Irving, snored peacefully as the first images emerged in the developer tray. A few years later, as mature dogs, they looked on with curiosity as our home began to acquire the tools and trappings of the bookbinder's craft. Over the succeeding years, as Sandy developed a full-fledged working studio, our dogs Jennifer, Lucy, Ursula, and Amy adapted themselves with devotion, each in their unique way, to the routines of the workday. To this day, Ursula'a photo adorns the outfeed end of the trusty Vandercook 219, where she would always station herself. Today, Sadie and Rose continue that tradition, and while production is occasionally slowed by an errant dog hair on an inked form, their loyal presence, their affection and bonding with Sandy's collaborators and assistants, and their reminders to take time for play and treats are an immeasurable asset to the press, and to our life together.

The second marker is a shared affinity. I have long been intrigued by the word *numinous*. While you can look it up in the dictionary, it remains in a sense indefinable, or perhaps it yields more meanings the more you consider it. I think it suggests the figurative campfire where Sandy and I first came together and where we continue to warm ourselves. I remember shortly after we met, Sandy described the struggles of a mathematical proof and the pleasure of reaching "the elegant solution," the crystalline insight that integrates the elements in the simplest, most economical way and gives a glimpse of the underlying order of things. Later, inspired by the work of Ansel Adams and Edward Weston, she used her camera and that homebuilt enlarger to search for revelation in the tones and textures of the world. The physical presence of books has its own divine mystery, and Sandy spent many years of hard work honoring that mystery. As she has ventured into the world of letterpress printing, in her bringing together of words and images, ink and paper, I continue to see her pursue the elegant solution that allows a glimpse of a larger reality, one that can be touched though not completely grasped by the senses. And I, who still look for the numinous in fugues, motets, and elevation toccatas, marvel at the fact that even though—in my personal opinion—she works too hard, she manages to have a great deal of fun in the process. Maybe that's one lesson we have from the dogs: if you're looking for revelation, you might as well revel!

— PATRICK TILCOCK

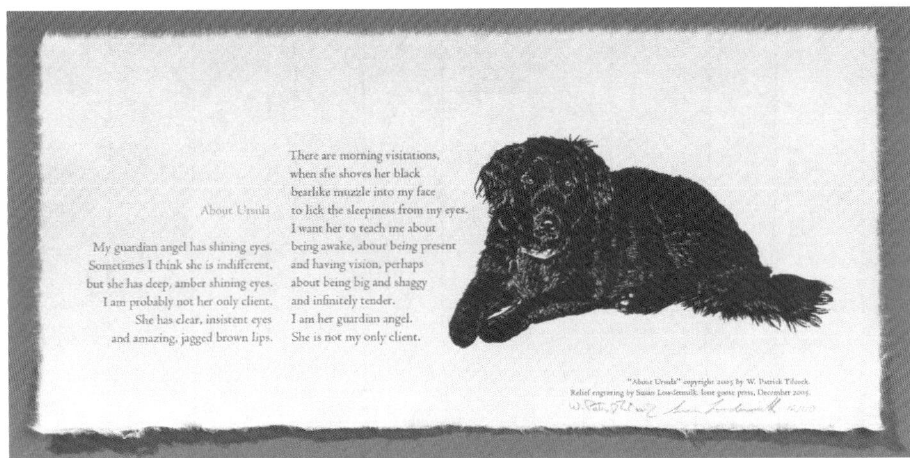

LGP15

lone goose press 1989–2013

lone goose press was launched in the fall of 1989 when friends Allyn Kersnar and David Bryant were visiting from New Zealand. The recently acquired Vandercook 219 was finally operational and I had acquired a small amount of used Caslon types. The three of us decided to print a keepsake, "Littoral Interpretation," in three days.

The name lone goose press is derived from the first book project, "March: The Geese Return", an excerpt from *A Sand County Almanac* by Aldo Leopold, that I did as a student. In that excerpt Leopold observes: "watching the daily routine of a spring goose convention, one notices the prevalence of singles—lone geese that do much flying about and much talking. One is apt to impute a disconsolate tone to their honkings . . . goose flocks are families, and lone geese in spring . . . are . . . bereaved survivors of the winter's shooting, searching in vain for their kin." Leaving my fellow classmates at Alabama, folks with whom I shared the love and passion for making books, left me a bit "bereaved." It would be several years before the community of Eugene, Oregon, would embrace what I was trying to do.

lone goose press is all lowercase because, as a former calligrapher, I wanted to leave open the option to play with the lowercase g, allowing its descender to "fly."

It has been the mission of lone goose press to promote book arts, to celebrate outstanding writing and to foster conversation about community, social justice, and environmental ethics.

Unless otherwise indicated, all publications of lone goose press have been printed using an old-style Vandercook 219 proof press, manufactured in 1940.

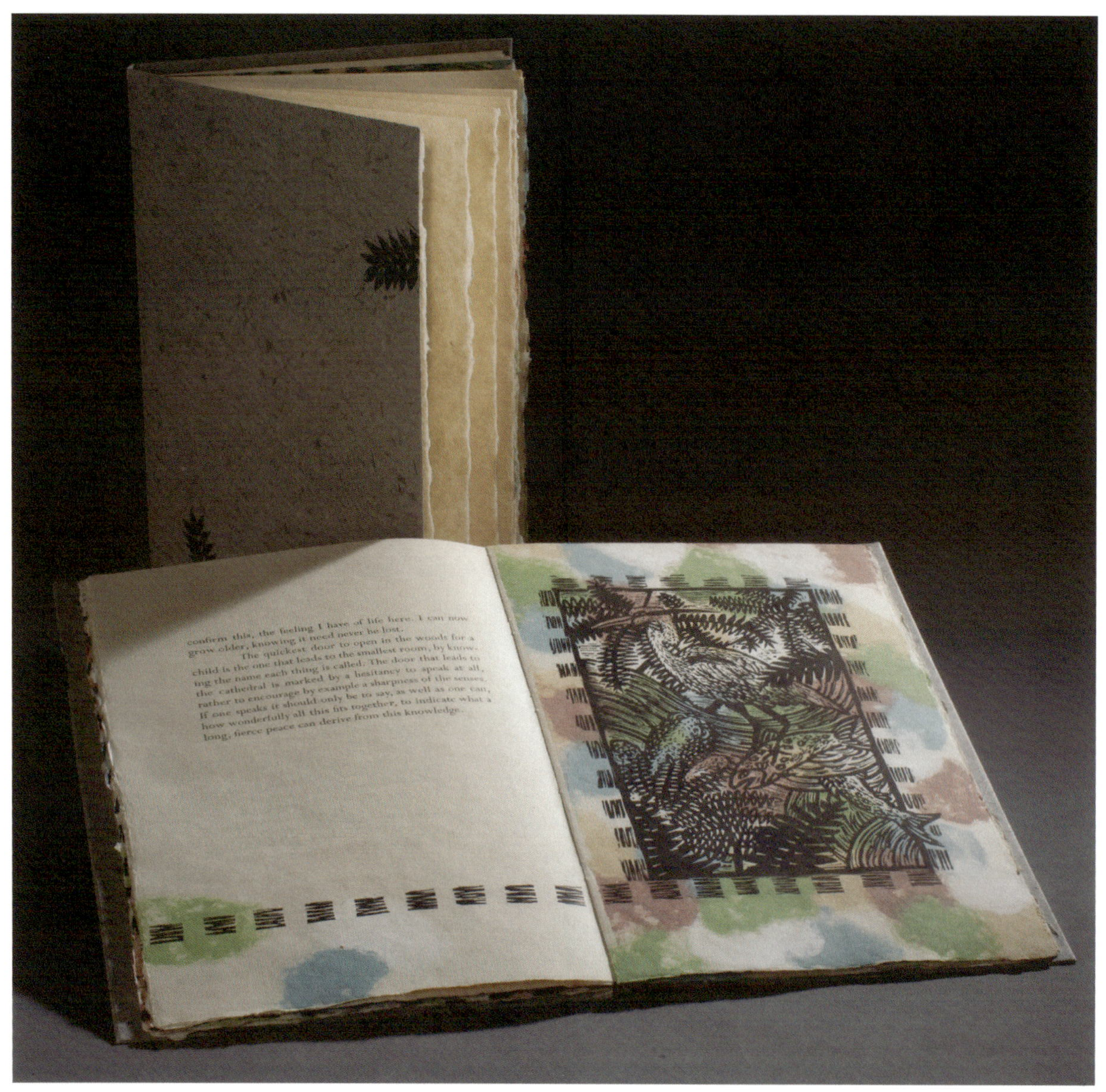
confirm this, the feeling I have of life here. I can now
grow older, knowing it need never be lost.
The quickest door to open in the woods for a
child is the one that leads to the smallest room, by knowing the name each thing is called. The door that leads to
the cathedral is marked by a hesitancy to speak at all,
rather to encourage by example a sharpness of the senses.
If one speaks it should only be to say, as well as one can,
how wonderfully all this fits together, to indicate what a
long, fierce peace can derive from this knowledge.

LGP1

LONE GOOSE PRESS BOOKS

LGP1 **Children in the Woods (1992)**

Barry Lopez
Linocuts by Margaret Prentice
Image on page 12

12.2 x 8 inches, 20 pages

75 copies numbered and signed by the author and the artist

Handset Perpetua types

Title lettering and opening initial hand-drawn by Marilyn Reaves and reproduced using magnesium plates

Text and cover papers made by Margaret Prentice from the plant fiber abaca with patterns created in the paper's body using colored pulp

Sewn binding with a supported paper wrapper, housed in a clamshell box using a forest green book cloth

There were also five lettered copies signed by the author and artist but not mentioned in the colophon. A printed note indicates that lone goose press bought back those unbound copies from the author for a nominal fee, binding them for sale as a special issue to benefit the press—a considerate gesture on the part of the author.

This was the first major publication from lone goose press and marked the beginning of a long friendship as well as a working relationship with Barry. I had never met Barry but a mutual friend arranged for a lunch meeting. At this meeting I shared with Barry my work from graduate school and my vision for a publishing press. At that time he let me know that he would go home, look for an appropriate manuscript, and have his agent draw up a contract. At the time of the meeting I had neither a press nor type but I did not let on to him that that was the case. Only later (much later) did he realize I was sharing a dream with him. Once completed, the book was an immediate success and lone goose press was launched. I am forever indebted to Barry for his patience with the project and his guidance throughout. He taught me much about publishing and about striving for excellence.

"These settings are grounded in love, not commerce."

I began working with Sandy Tilcock as a writer in the fall of 1991, collaborating with her and the artist Margaret Prentice on a fine press book called *Children in the Woods*. At the time I knew very little about limited editions, let alone Twinrocker handmade papers or such things as sewing frames and composing sticks. I've had the privilege since then of being able to work with skilled artisans and visual artists at other fine presses around the country and have learned a lot from them, including how to stay out of the way. My criteria for judging the quality of a handmade book, though, were established in that initial experience with Sandy. One valuable thing I learned from her was the need to distinguish between what was exemplary work and what was merely good work when examining fine press limited edition books.

Sandy never wanted anything to leave her studio that couldn't stand shoulder-to-shoulder with the best work being done. One needs more nuanced adjectives than "painstaking" or "meticulous" to convey what she was up to. She was not a fanatic, but if a slipcase she was working on developed a flaw, she would simply set it aside and begin again with new materials. If the inking on the rollers of her Vandercook 219 was uneven—and no matter that this problem was not apparent to anyone but her—she would clean the rollers and start over. She identified with this kind of striving. It took her work beyond the ordinary.

Less and less do people pursue this kind of exceptionalism today, especially in work where the unaided human hand is the primary tool, and where the tools themselves are as simple as a bone folder or an X-acto knife. This sort of work requires ferocious concentration and precision. I've watched Sandy listening to her press during a run to check on the tackiness of the ink and seen her sewing in headbands like she was doing eye surgery. When one enters a fine press studio like hers—the physical landscape of the limited edition book, of deckle-edged chapbooks and letterpress broadsides—the quality of the air seems to change. The deep history of this object, the book, becomes more mysterious. And the role of the printed word in keeping alive the small, imperiled fires of Western cultural aspiration becomes more apparent.

For a writer, to work alongside someone like Sandy is to understand a new dimension of storytelling, one that offers a continuous through line to the past, from the glass-fronted shelves of the Pierpont Morgan Library in New York today to the ghost of the incinerated library at Alexandria, a line that includes, too, settings like a clear patch of snow in the Arctic, where Inuit families gather to watch and listen while a storyteller draws on the wind-burnished surface with a storyteller's knife. These settings are grounded in love, not commerce. In each setting, the concern for the fate of others is clear. And with each handmade book, each codex closely examined, a feeling of awe rises up as the attributes of natural materials become known to the tips of the finger — the tooth of a mould-made paper, the texture of goatskin; and as the ear and the nose become more aware — the crackle of a parchment page, the aromatics of glue and ink.

The making of beautiful, enduring work and the celebration of storytelling have been Sandy's calling for nearly thirty years. You hold here the record of what she has accomplished. How can anyone ask more of a person than what she has given us? And how can you not marvel at the uncomplicated and straightforward perfection of an artisan who sees a world larger than herself?

Along with other writers in this list who have said this, I want to acknowledge how good Sandy's work has made me look, and speak, like them, of the great honor we all feel at having been included within the ambit of her excellence.

— BARRY LOPEZ

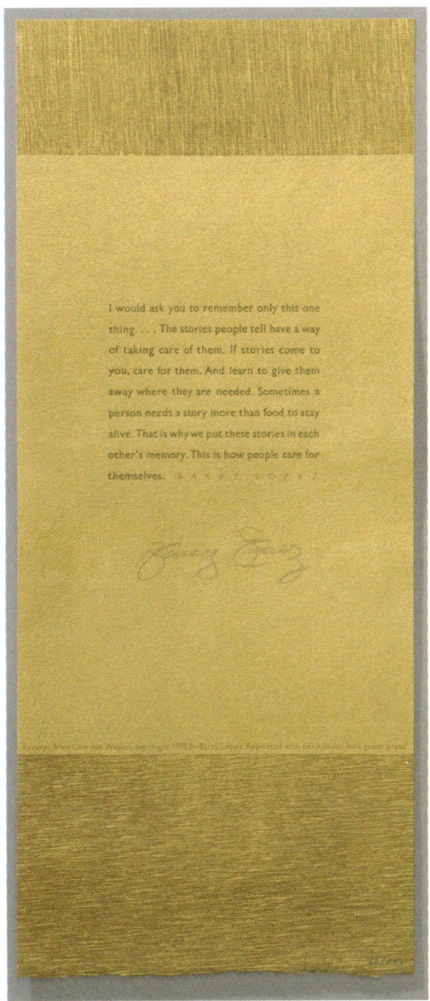

LGP13

LGP2 **Apple Bough Soliloquy (1995)**

Kim Stafford
Woodcuts by Susan Lowdermilk

6.7 x 6.4 inches, 28 pages

100 numbered copies, 26 lettered copies, signed by the author and the artist

Title lettering and opening initial hand-drawn by Marilyn Reaves and reproduced using magnesium plates

Handset Perpetua types

Arches Text Wove paper

Case binding in quarter cloth with paste papers by Sandy Tilcock over boards; title label on spine

Lettered copies presented in a box and accompanied by a print of the book's double-page image on handmade paper and signed by the artist

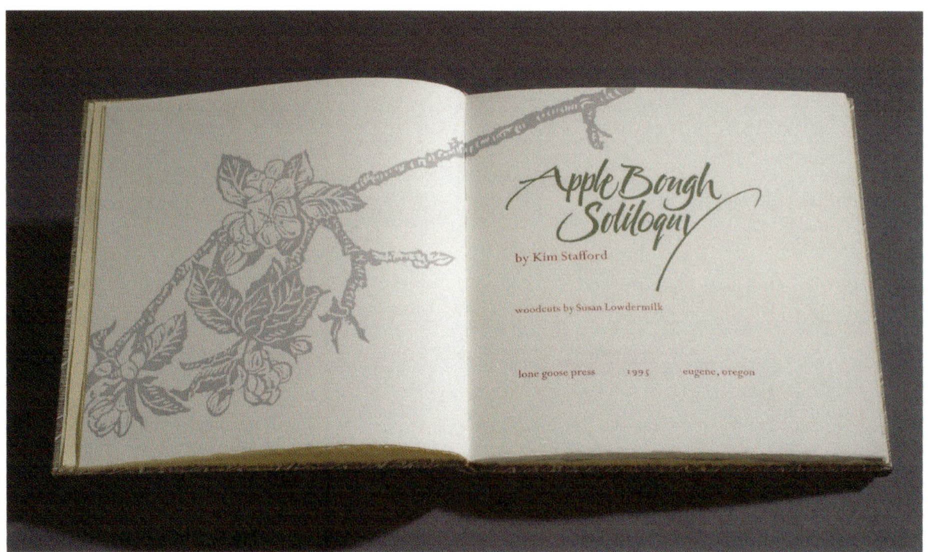

LGP2

LGP3 **Looking in a Deeper Lair: A Tribute to Wallace Stegner (1996)**

Barry Lopez
Intaglio print by Suellen Larkin in deluxe copies

6.5 x 9.6 inches, 22 pages

150 numbered softcover copies, 29 deluxe hardcover copies of which 26 are lettered, and three are designated as artist's copies; all copies are signed by the author and the deluxe copies are also signed by the artist

Handset Perpetua types

Zerkall German Ingres paper

Softcover bindings are a supported paper wrapper using grigio Fabriano Ingres (cover)

Deluxe copies bound in quarter cloth (red mohair) with Twinrocker handmade paper over boards and presented in a clamshell box covered in red mohair book cloth

The essay, which originally appeared in *Northern Lights*, is based on remarks Barry made at the Herbst Theatre in San Francisco on April 27, 1995, when he joined Ivan Doig, Gretel Ehrlich, William Kittredge, Page Stegner, and Terry Tempest Williams in an evening of testimony to honor Wallace Stegner. The essay won a 1996 Pushcart Prize for essays.

LGP4 **Thinking Like a Mountain (1990)**

Aldo Leopold
Woodcut by Diane Tarter

16.5 x 22 inches

60 numbered copies signed by the artist

Handset Caslon types

Taupe Amora paper

Excerpt from *A Sand County Almanac and Sketches Here and There*, Aldo Leopold (Oxford University Press, 1949)

Printed on back: The collaborators wish to acknowledge that the broadside contains a typographic error. The eighth line should read, 'that no wolves would mean hunters' paradise.' We hope the reader will accept our apologies for this 'humility stitch.'

LGP5 **After Arguing against the Contention That Art Must Come from Discontent (1991)**

William Stafford
Linocut by Susan Lowdermilk

18.5 x 13.5 inches

100 numbered and 26 lettered copies signed by the author and the artist

Handset Centaur types

Rives BFK paper, hand-dyed dark blue by Susan Kristoferson

The first in a series of broadsides printed in conjunction with the Lane Arts Council's annual Voices of Place reading series. A portion of the proceeds from the sales of this broadside was donated to the Lane Arts Council. The 26 lettered copies were housed in folders and presented to the artists and donors who made the project possible.

LGP6 **I Pray to the Birds** (1992)

Terry Tempest Williams
Brush lettering by Marilyn Reaves reproduced using magnesium plates

9.7 x 16.6 inches

100 numbered and 26 lettered copies signed by the author and artist

Handset Perpetua types

Printed on handmade paper from the Velké Losiny paper mill in the Czech Republic

Brush lettering enhanced by gold and iridescent green pigments applied by hand while the ink was wet

Excerpt from *Refuge: An Unnatural History of Family and Place,* Terry Tempest Williams (Pantheon Books, 1991)

The second in a series of broadsides printed in conjunction with the Lane Arts Council's annual Voices of Place reading series. A portion of the proceeds from the sales of this broadside was donated to the Lane Arts Council. The 26 lettered copies were housed in folders and presented to the artists and donors who made the project possible.

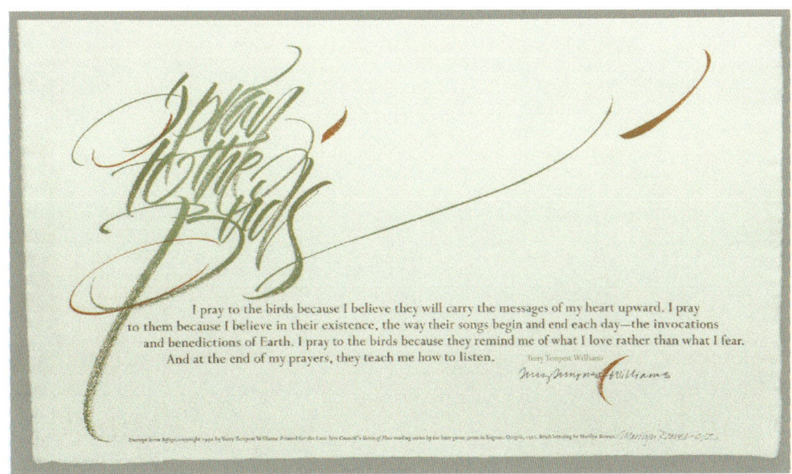

LGP6

LGP7 **The First Thing About Rocks Is, They're Old (1993)**

Ursula K. Le Guin
Calligraphy by Edie Roberts reproduced using magnesium plates

12.3 inches diameter, circular format

85 numbered copies signed by the author

Handset Perpetua types

Dampened handmade paper from India that is 100 percent cotton and colored with ash

Circle hand-torn after final print run

Excerpt from *Buffalo Gals and Other Animal Presences,* Ursula K. Le Guin (Capra Press, 1987)

The third in a series of broadsides printed in conjunction with the Lane Arts Council's annual Voices of Place reading series. A portion of the proceeds from the sales of this broadside was donated to the Lane Arts Council. Ten of the copies were housed in folders and presented to the artists and donors who made the project possible.

LGP8 **Bristlecones (1994)**

Stephen Trimble
Wood engraving by Susan Lowdermilk
Image on page 21

9 x 7 inches folded (tri-fold), 9 x 20.9 inches unfolded

50 numbered copies signed by the author and the artist

Handset Perpetua types

Hand-drawn initial by Allyn Kersnar reproduced using magnesium plate

Handmade cogon grass paper from the Philippines

Tri-fold is hand-torn at top and bottom with bottom folded back to form a landscape; presented in a paper envelope made from Canson Mi-Teintes

Excerpt from *The Sagebrush Ocean: A Natural History of the Great Basin,* Stephen Trimble (University of Nevada Press, 1989)

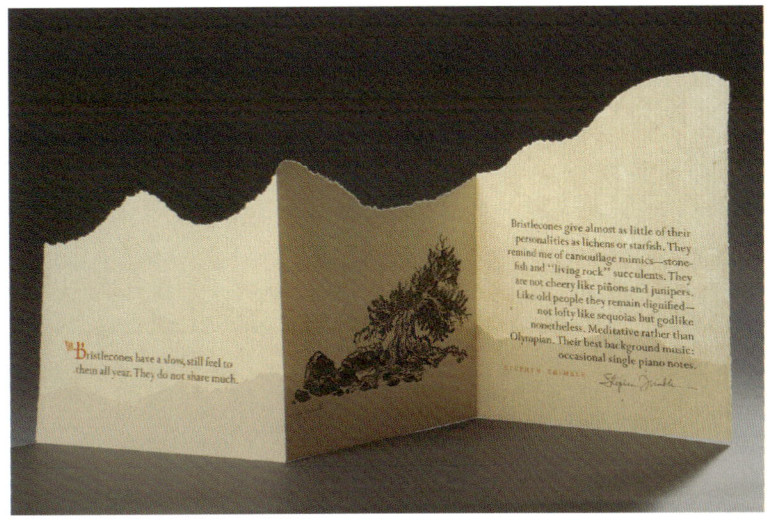

LGP8

LGP9 **Thanksgiving at Snake Butte (1994)**

James Welch
Linocut by Sandy and Patrick Tilcock

17 x 10½ inches

85 numbered copies signed by the author

Handset Centaur types

Dampened handmade flax paper from J.B. Green of England

Linocut derived from an incised boulder in the Wees Bar petroglyph field on the Snake River in southwestern Idaho

James Welch was primarily a fiction writer. His first published book—and his only book of poetry—is *Riding the Earthboy 40* (World Publishing, 1971), where this poem appears.

This is the fourth broadside printed in conjunction with the Lane Arts Council's annual Voices of Place series. A portion of the proceeds from the sales of this broadside was donated to the Lane Arts Council.

LGP10 **The Eye of Time** **(1996)**

Ivan Doig
Woodcut by Susan Lowdermilk

10 x 14.3 inches

100 numbered copies signed by the author and the artist

Handset Perpetua types

Gray Rives BFK paper

Excerpt from the preface to *Inside this House of Sky: Photographs of a Western Landscape* by Duncan Kelso and Ivan Doig (Atheneum, 1983)

The fifth broadside printed in conjunction with the Lane Arts Council's annual Voices of Place series. A portion of the proceeds from the sales of this broadside was donated to the Lane Arts Council.

LGP11 **Opus from Space** **(1998)**

Pattiann Rogers
Drawing by Judith Sparks reproduced using a magnesium plate

20 x 12 inches

75 numbered copies signed by the author and the artist

Handset Centaur types

Twinrocker handmade paper

LGP12 **Wild Mercy** **(2003)**

Terry Tempest Williams
Brush lettering by Marilyn Reaves reproduced using a polymer plate

13 x 9.8 inches

120 numbered copies signed by the author

White Somerset Velvet paper

Brush lettering printed "in blind"

Excerpt from *Red Passion and Patience in the Desert,* Terry Tempest Williams (Pantheon Books, 2001)

LGP13 **I Would Ask You to Remember This One Thing (2004)**

Barry Lopez
Wood grain graphics by Sandy Tilcock
Image on page 15

15 x 6.5 inches

100 numbered copies signed by the author

Handset Gill Sans type

Yatsuo paper from Japan consisting of kozo fiber

Excerpt from *Crow and Weasel,* Barry Lopez (North Point Press, 1990)

LGP14 **We Regard Ourselves as Servants of Memory (2005)**

Barry Lopez
Graphic by Sandy Tilcock, created from compressed text of the Declaration of Independence

11.5 x 10 inches

100 numbered copies signed by the author

Handset Gill Sans type

Hahnemühle Bugra paper

Excerpt from "Apocalypse," which appears in *Resistance*, Barry Lopez (Knopf, 2004)

LGP15 **About Ursula (2005)**

W. Patrick Tilcock
Relief engraving by Susan Lowdermilk
Image on page 9

6 x 12.8 inches

110 numbered copies signed by the author and the artist

Handset Centaur types

Mulberry paper from Japan

Hand-coloring in engraving by Sandy Tilcock

Ursula (1995–2005) positioned herself at the foot of the press upon her first visit to lone goose press as a six-week-old puppy. Her sheer delight in welcoming visitors soon earned her the title "Director of Public Relations." Memories of Ursula: her disarming habit of licking the bare knees of the UPS delivery person and other guests, her conversations with writer Barry Lopez, her deftly hiding rawhide chews under the studio equipment in order to taunt her canine sisters. Primarily, we will remember the joy and laughter she brought to our lives.

LGP16 **Crossing the Willamette (2006)**

W. Patrick Tilcock
Brush drawing by Marilyn Reaves reproduced using a polymer plate

12.3 x 7 inches

87 numbered copies signed by the author and the artist

Handset Perpetua types

Nideggen paper

Brush lettering hand-colored by Marilyn Reaves

Printed to honor the friends and supporters of lone goose press and to celebrate the completion of the press's new home on Augusta Street. It was also the beginning of lone goose press using prime numbers for its edition sizes.

LGP17 **Call and Answer (2006)**

Robert Bly
Woodcut by Susan Lowdermilk

12 x 12 inches

97 numbered copies signed by the author and the artist

Handset Gill Sans type

Somerset Book paper

Printed in conjunction with Robert Bly's visit to Eugene, Oregon, in October 2006.

lone goose press dedicated the broadside to the memory of William Stafford and his advocacy for peace.

LGP18 **To the Book (2007)**

W. S. Merwin
Collagraph of a historical typographic ornament by Sandy Tilcock
Image on page 35

13 x 6.3 inches

113 numbered copies signed by the author

Handset Centaur types

Somerset Book paper

The broadside was published to commemorate the July 21, 2007, opening of an exhibit at the Collins Gallery, Multnomah County Library, Portland, Oregon, in celebration of the 35th anniversary of Copper Canyon Press, which has published poetry exclusively and has established an international reputation for its commitment to authors, editorial acumen, and dedication to the poetry audience.

“The text will always be the organizing principle . . . ”

I have watched Sandy’s work for decades and count myself fortunate to have worked collaboratively with her on several book and broadside projects. When I was employed at the Oregon College of Art and Craft, Sandy came as a guest instructor in Book Arts to teach a course in box construction.

Immediately, I was impressed with the thoroughness of her preparation, her standards, her expectations, and her inventive approach to both book and box structures. When she showed examples of her past work it was evident that Sandy, as designer, typographer, and bookbinder, had a graceful, light aesthetic that supported the message of the selected text.

For me, this is what makes Sandy’s work singular in the field of handmade books and broadsides. In all of her projects she seeks the elegant, thoughtful presentation of an author’s words. The text will always be the organizing principle in all phases of a project Sandy undertakes — not the images, fonts, papers, decorations, or binding. Her humility in treating and interpreting an author’s words is to be admired.

From the beginning of each project the conversation between us was respectful and inclusive of one another’s ideas. We devoted plenty of time to the “what if” stage of envisioning the shape of the project. Thumbnails, drawings, test pages, etc. evolved from our back and forth deliberations.

Together we used our unique talents to support and present an author’s work. Collaboration has become a shop-worn term in the world of art. The trend has been to anoint a project that involves more than one artist with the warm and fuzzy word “collaboration,” to imply that each artist involved did an equal amount of the thinking and the work to produce something outstanding. Often the desired result is lost in a struggle of participant egos.

Sandy is clear about her leadership and goals with a project. She is a text-driven artist and craftswoman. Like a symphony conductor with an orchestra, she brings all of her experience, vision, and skill to bear on producing a transcendent piece of art. When we worked together we always wanted to do something new and challenging. We have definitely had a few adventures which lengthened the process, but we were never sorry that we pursued new ideas.

— MARGOT VOORHIES THOMPSON

LGP19 **Dependence Day** **(2007)**

John Daniel
Brush artwork by Margot Voorhies Thompson reproduced using a polymer plate

18 x 11.5 inches

103 numbered copies signed by the author and the artist

Handset Perpetua types

Black Somerset Velvet paper

Upper part of artwork dusted with silver pearl dry pigment while the ink was wet

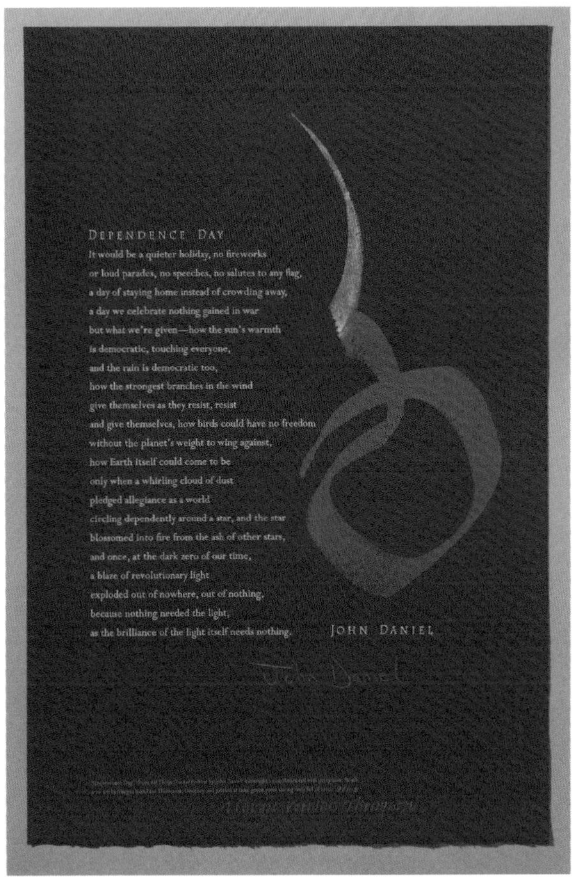

DEPENDENCE DAY

It would be a quieter holiday, no fireworks
or loud parades, no speeches, no salutes to any flag,
a day of staying home instead of crowding away,
a day we celebrate nothing gained in war
but what we're given—how the sun's warmth
is democratic, touching everyone,
and the rain is democratic too,
how the strongest branches in the wind
give themselves as they resist, resist
and give themselves, how birds could have no freedom
without the planet's weight to wing against,
how Earth itself could come to be
only when a whirling cloud of dust
pledged allegiance as a world
circling dependently around a star, and the star
blossomed into fire from the ash of other stars,
and once, at the dark zero of our time,
a blaze of revolutionary light
exploded out of nowhere, out of nothing,
because nothing needed the light,
as the brilliance of the light itself needs nothing.

JOHN DANIEL

LGP19

LGP20 **Perhaps the World Ends Here (2008)**

Joy Harjo

Drawing by Bob DeVine and reproduced as a giclée print with the red added by hand

13 x 19.4 inches

101 numbered copies signed by the author and the artist

Handset Gill Sans types in the poem; display type computer-set Charlemagne reproduced using a polymer plate

Off-white Rives BFK paper

Original pencil drawing by Bob DeVine scanned, reduced, and printed on an Epson 4880 inkjet

lone goose press wishes to thank the Celebration Foundation of Portland, Oregon, for the grant that made the acquisition of the Epson 4880 possible.

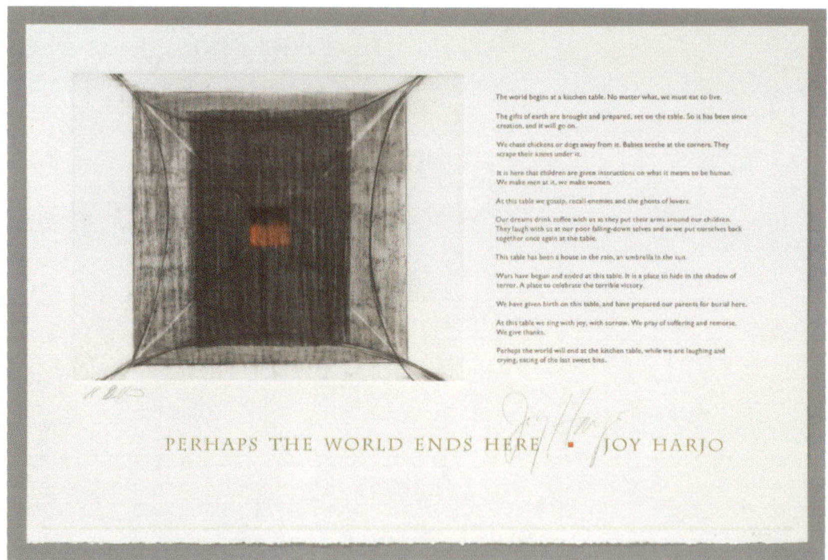

LGP20

LGP21 **Evidence Suggests That Dirt Is Beneficial To Your Health — For Sandy (2008)**

W. Patrick Tilcock
Background photograph by W. Patrick Tilcock

16 x 7.5 inches

83 numbered copies signed by the author

Computer-set Optima types printed using polymer plates

Handmade Kitakata paper from Japan

Background image derived from a digital photograph and printed with an Epson 4880 inkjet printer

LGP22 **Famous (2008)**

Naomi Shihab Nye
Enso image from the press archives reproduced using a polymer plate
Image on page vi

17 x 10.4 inches

97 numbered copies signed by the author

Computer-set Optima types printed using polymer plates

Canal paper (Sisal Coffee) from the Saint-Armand paper mill in Montreal, Canada, made using a variety of recycled fibers

Poem from *The Words Under the Words: Selected Poems,* Naomi Shihab Nye (Eighth Mountain Press, A Far Corner Book, 1995)

The broadside is dedicated to the memory of Michael DeRobertis, who graced the lives of many in his community.

LGP23 **Mercy, Tear It Down (2009)**

Michael McGriff
Drawings by Keith Achepohl reproduced using polymer plates
Image on page 32

19.8 x 13.3 inches

107 numbered copies signed by the author and the artist

Computer-set Gill Sans for the poem and Charlemagne Bold for the display

Gray cotton Canal paper from the Saint-Armand mill in Montreal, Canada, made using a variety of recycled fibers

LGP24 **Cross of Iron (2009)**

Dwight D. Eisenhower

14.3 x 7 inches

131 numbered copies

Handset Optima type

Somerset Book paper

Excerpt from "The Chance for Peace," a speech Eisenhower delivered before the American Society of Newspaper Editors on April 16, 1953

This broadside is dedicated to the memory of William Stafford, whose advocacy for peace was never-ending.

In spring 2002, the lone goose press printed an unnumbered edition of this excerpt that was distributed as a gift to visitors and friends of the press. The unnumbered edition is the same except the phrase "those who hunger and are not fed" is omitted from the 2002 printing.

LGP25 **Our Flag** (2011)

Carl Adamshick
Artwork by Keith Achepohl

25 x 8.3 inches

53 numbered copies signed by the author and the artist

Computer-set Kabel type printed using polymer plates

Seikosen paper made by Shigeru Ozaki in Kochi prefecture, using Japanese Mitsumata that is cultivated in the local mountains surrounding the Ozaki home

Original artwork consisted of line drawings and etchings; the etchings were scanned and digitally manipulated to create relief plates to render the flag textures

LGP26 **Prayer** (2012)

Tom Crawford
Artwork by Bob DeVine
Image on page 33

20.5 x 17 inches

79 numbered copies signed by the author and the artist

Computer-set Optima types; Donatello for display type; printed using polymer plates

Kitakata paper, handmade in Japan using Gampi fiber

Original pencil drawing by Bob DeVine scanned, a photopolymer intaglio plate made and printed on an etching press

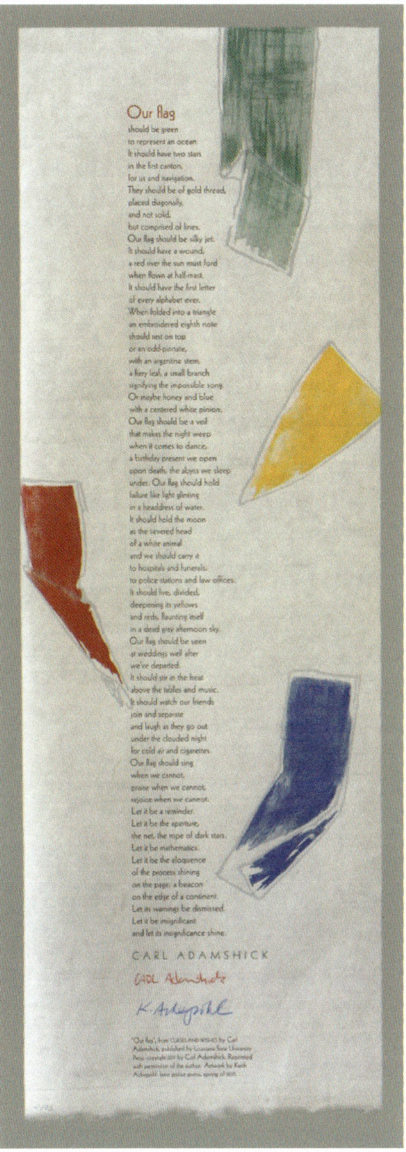

LGP25

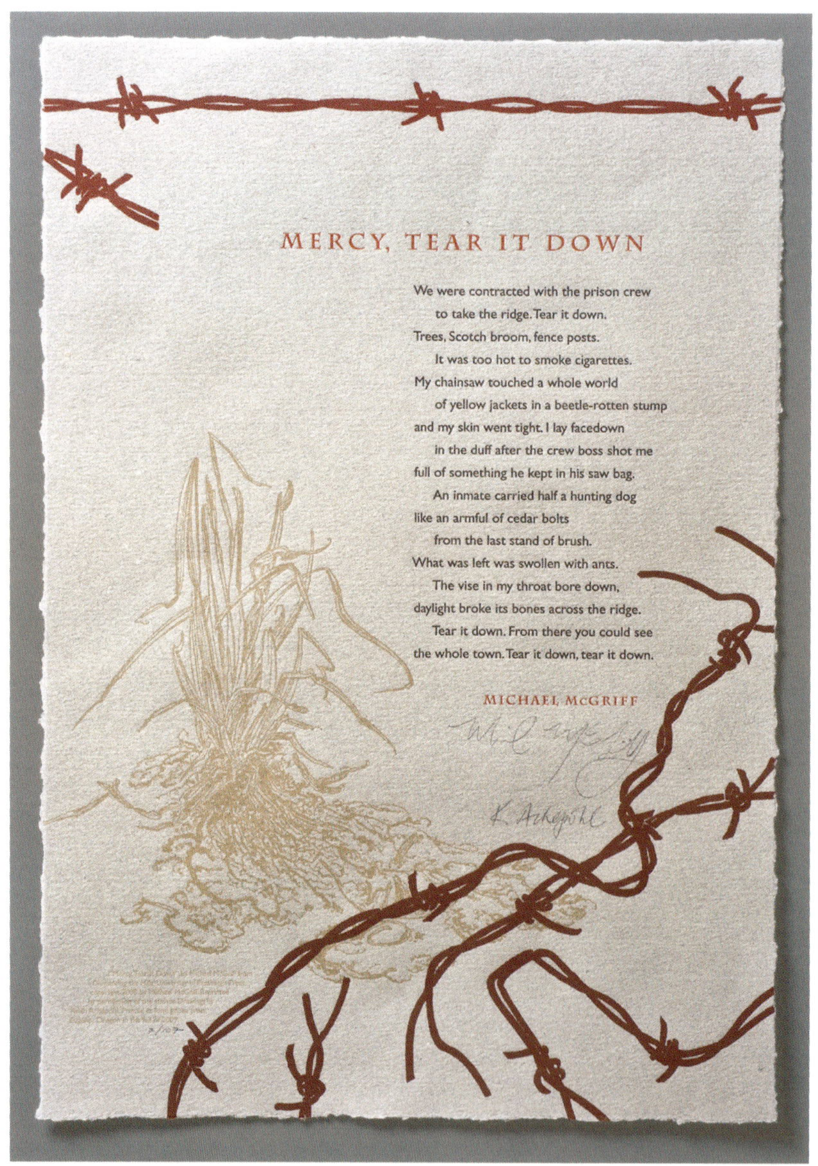
MERCY, TEAR IT DOWN
We were contracted with the prison crew
to take the ridge. Tear it down.
Trees, Scotch broom, fence posts.
It was too hot to smoke cigarettes.
My chainsaw touched a whole world
of yellow jackets in a beetle-rotten stump
and my skin went tight. I lay facedown
in the duff after the crew boss shot me
full of something he kept in his saw bag.
An inmate carried half a hunting dog
like an armful of cedar bolts
from the last stand of brush.
What was left was swollen with ants.
The vise in my throat bore down,
daylight broke its bones across the ridge.
Tear it down. From there you could see
the whole town. Tear it down, tear it down.
MICHAEL McGRIFF

LGP23

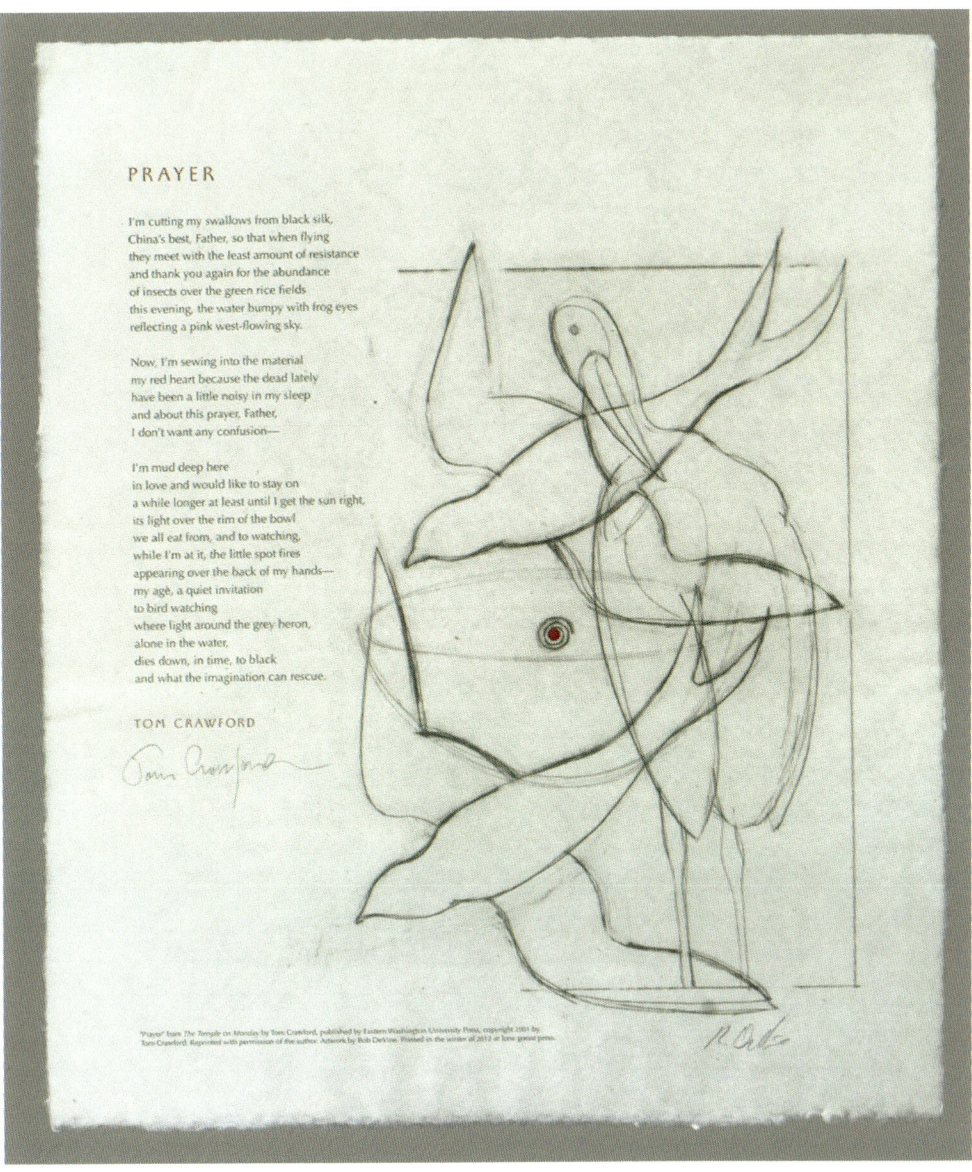

PRAYER

I'm cutting my swallows from black silk,
China's best, Father, so that when flying
they meet with the least amount of resistance
and thank you again for the abundance
of insects over the green rice fields
this evening, the water bumpy with frog eyes
reflecting a pink west-flowing sky.

Now, I'm sewing into the material
my red heart because the dead lately
have been a little noisy in my sleep
and about this prayer, Father,
I don't want any confusion—

I'm mud deep here
in love and would like to stay on
a while longer at least until I get the sun right,
its light over the rim of the bowl
we all eat from, and to watching,
while I'm at it, the little spot fires
appearing over the back of my hands—
my age, a quiet invitation
to bird watching
where light around the grey heron,
alone in the water,
dies down, in time, to black
and what the imagination can rescue.

TOM CRAWFORD

"Prayer" from *The Temple on Monday* by Tom Crawford, published by Eastern Washington University Press, copyright 2001 by Tom Crawford. Reprinted with permission of the author. Artwork by Bob DeVine. Printed in the winter of 2012 at lone goose press.

LGP26

"...a stubborn refusal to be imperfect."

When I consider Sandy Tilcock and the work that she's done at her lone goose press, as I handle the hundreds of pieces of paper, notebooks, polymer plates, binding models, correspondence, and objects diverse and lovely as the warmly inscribed broadsides by writers who are at the pinnacle of their craft to objects that are as obtuse and dangerous as barbed wire—all part of her archives at the John Wilson Special Collections—I want to say that Sandy's a rock star.

But she may not be loud enough to be a rock star.

Connecting her to the father of the private press movement, William Morris, is perhaps more fitting. Morris, who died in 1896, brought his brilliant vision to the book world with his Kelmscott Press, producing beautiful books of the highest quality. He chose the handmade papers, the particular typefaces, the authors and texts he wished to publish, the illustrators he thought best to accompany these words, and the bindings necessary to make his books the sought-after items they remain today.

And he did it with great care, grace, diligence, and a stubborn refusal to be imperfect.

And that describes Sandy Tilcock's work, too. Except, unlike William Morris, who simply but thankfully had the vision of these books and had the finest craftsmen of his day actually make them, Sandy Tilcock sets her own type, operates her own hand-press, and binds all of her books.

A rock star.

In the dozen years I've known Sandy Tilcock, I've watched her create wonderful publications, from the moment of their conception to their completion. I've hired her to produce intricate boxes to house treasures from the special collections I direct, including, fittingly, William Morris's grand Chaucer. I've served on the board of the Knight Library Press, where Sandy shifted her efforts from her private press to serve the University of Oregon for several years, and then returned to lone goose to continue her adventures in the way that she has chosen. And I was overjoyed when she told me she wanted my special collections to be the repository of her papers.

The John Wilson Special Collections serves many populations, but among its largest is the rich book arts community of Portland. For these visitors, especially the students from Oregon College of Art and Craft, Pacific Northwest College of Art, and Portland State University, having access to Sandy Tilcock's rich career as a fine press publisher is extraordinarily valuable. Not only can they handle the actual projects, dummies, printing samples, and ink swatches, they can read correspondence between Sandy and her authors; they can see publication costs on detailed price sheets created for each project; they can read her student notebooks that clearly reveal great techniques learned from extraordinary practitioners in the field, including Richard-Gabriel Rummonds. And they will be able to do this forever.

For all this, and because of Sandy Tilcock's generosity to share her work with all of us so freely, we are eternally grateful.

— JIM CARMIN

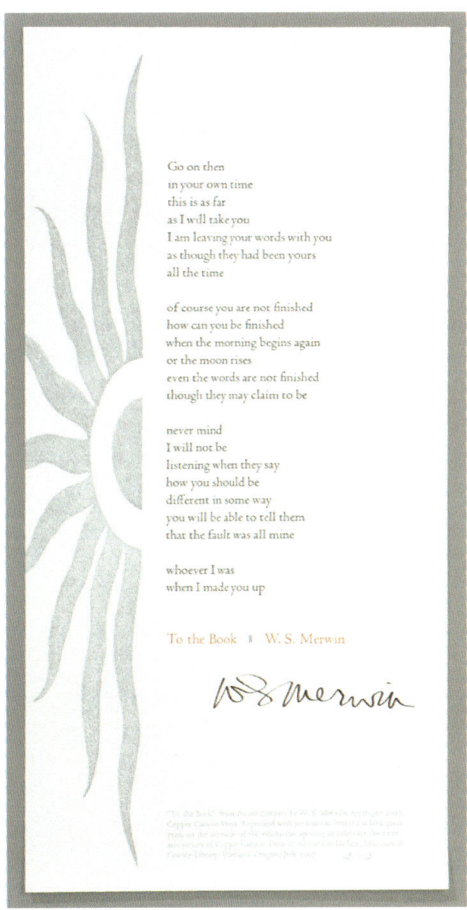

Go on then
in your own time
this is as far
as I will take you
I am leaving your words with you
as though they had been yours
all the time

of course you are not finished
how can you be finished
when the morning begins again
or the moon rises
even the words are not finished
though they may claim to be

never mind
I will not be
listening when they say
how you should be
different in some way
you will be able to tell them
that the fault was all mine

whoever I was
when I made you up

To the Book ▪ W. S. Merwin

LGP18

CAMBIUM BROADSIDE SERIES: 2008 –

The "Cambium Broadside Series" was created to honor the work of young writers. This series acknowledges the fresh insights of growing minds, and is dedicated to encouraging the art of writing in a new generation.

Cambium is a layer of formative cells between the bark and the hardwood. Each year the cambium produces additional wood and bark cells. This layer holds the potential for the future growth of the tree.

LGP27 **Snow (2008)**

Lucie Jane Carmin
Brush lettering of title by Marilyn Reaves reproduced using a polymer plate
Image on page 37

8.5 x 8.5 inches

71 numbered copies signed by the author

Handset Centaur types

Somerset Book paper

Poet is age 7

LGP28 **The Tallest Brother (2009)**

Zoe Duncan-Doroff
Graphic derived by Sandy Tilcock from photograph of shattered glass

14 x 6.3 inches

97 numbered copies signed by the author

Handset Gill Sans types

Zerkall Nideggen paper

Poet is age 10

Inspired by Liesel Mueller's poem "Night Song"

LGP29 **Eclipsed** (2010)

Dylan Troyer
Airbrushed graphic by Dale Jestice

10 x 10 inches

73 numbered copies signed by the author

Computer-set Stone Sans types printed using polymer plates

Somerset Velvet Black paper

Poet is age 10

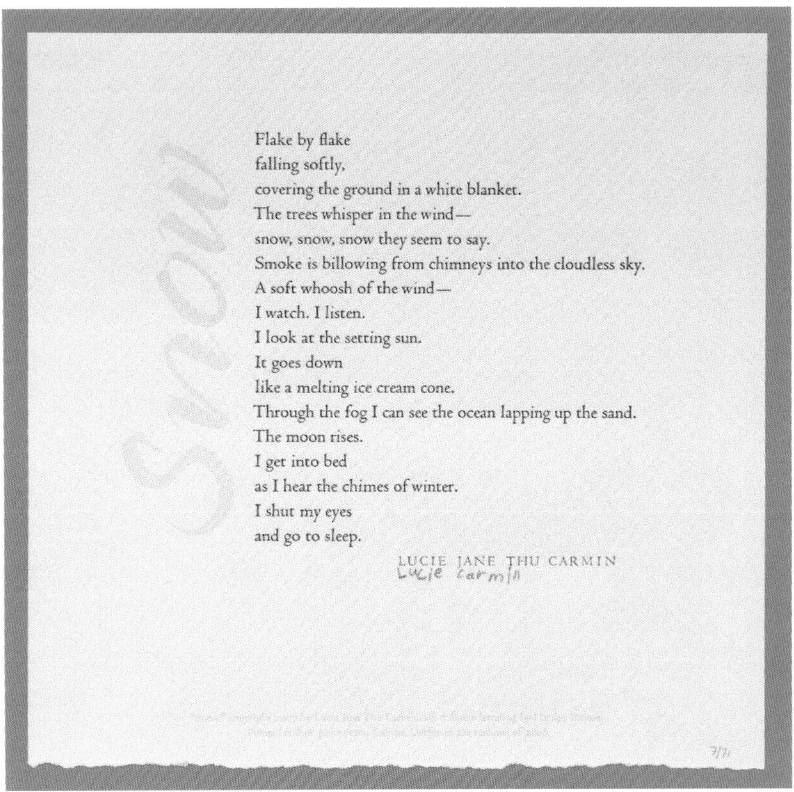

LGP27

PRAYER FLAG SERIES: 2010–

This project brings together brief pieces of writing by various authors in a format inspired by the Tibetan tradition of prayer flags. The writings may be new or excerpted from previous works. The authors were asked to consider the themes of hope, peace, reconciliation, and respect for nature. This effort springs from a desire to cultivate visions for the future that counterbalance the despair and cynicism that often seem to prevail in our society. There is no end date for this series, and the number of writings is not specified. The edition size of each flag will not exceed 97 copies. All the flags have the same format: an 8 x 8 inch square of Japanese paper on which the text is printed. This is then sewn to a 10 x 10 inch square of cloth custom-batiked with an enso image. The cloth is hemmed to form a loop at the top edge to accommodate a string to be used for hanging.

A hinged-lid box is available for storing the series. The box is covered in black mohair cloth and has black closing clasps handmade in India of buffalo bone. A window in the front of the box allows for a printed label mounted on a shallow pedestal. The box has a tray within a tray so that the strings are accommodated without their lying on the flag.

LGP30 **All Rights Reserved (2010)**

W. Patrick Tilcock

8 x 8 inches

83 numbered copies signed by the author

Computer-set Optima types; Beata for the display type; printed using polymer plates

Yatsuo paper from Japan consisting of Kozo fiber

This poem was printed in 2009 as a small keepsake which is entered as LGP37 on page 44.

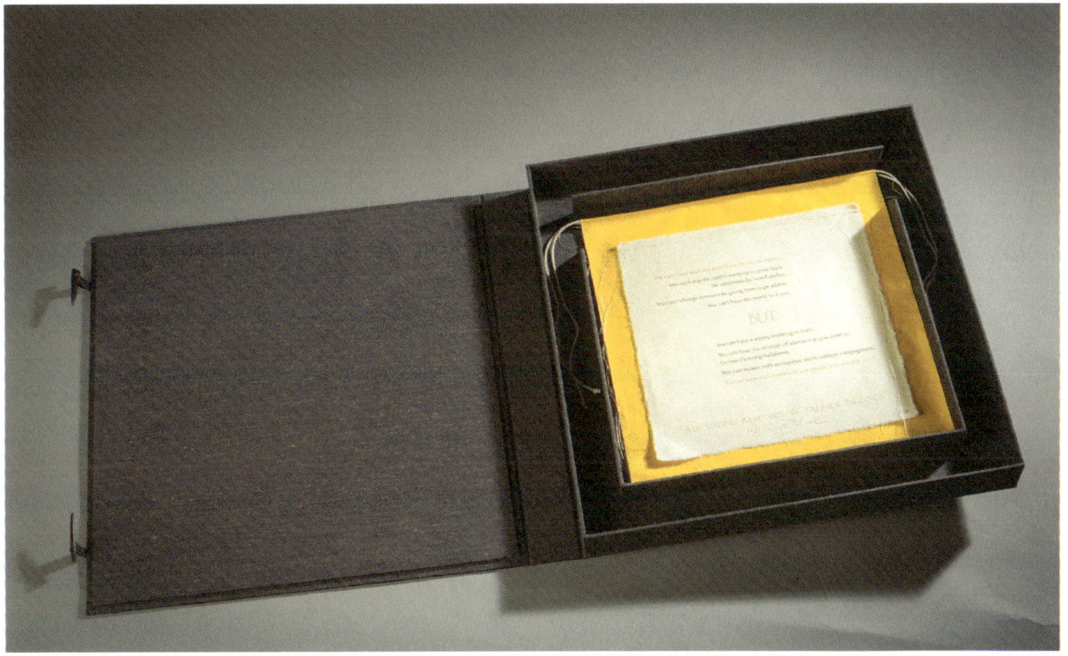

LGP30

LGP31 **We Belong to a Mystery (2010)**

John Daniel

8 x 8 inches

97 numbered copies signed by the author

Computer-set Albertus MT Pro type printed using polymer plates

Handmade paper from Thailand with lotus leaf watermark

Excerpt from *Winter Creek: One Writer's Natural History,* John Daniel (Milkweed Editions, 2002)

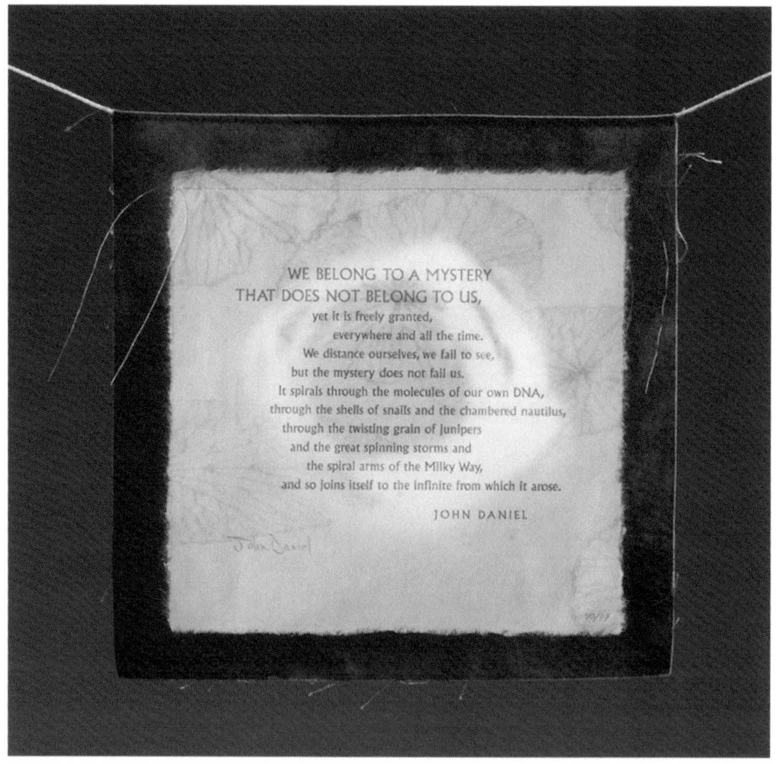

LGP31

LONE GOOSE PRESS EPHEMERA

LGP32 **Littoral Interpretation (1989)**

Patrick Tilcock
Linocut by David Bryant

7.5 x 5.3 inches, 4 pages

75 copies signed by the author

Handset Caslon type

Sekishu paper

Pamphlet sewing with Canson cover paper

Bubble printing on the cover paper by Sandy Tilcock and Allyn Kersnar

Presented in an envelope with bubble printing on the front

This keepsake is the first publication of lone goose press.

LGP33 **Winter Meditation Journal Entry: 12 February, 1990 (1991)**

Patrick Tilcock
Drawings of snowflakes by Patrick Tilcock

Title and initial letter calligraphy by Edie Roberts

6.9 x 4.3 inches, 4 pages

140 numbered copies, unsigned

Handset Perpetua type

Gray Amora paper

French fold pamphlet binding, sewn into Nero Fabriano Ingres covers

A snowflake image is in the background of the text and another snowflake image is on the cover.

Printed in memory of Patrick Tilcock's grandfather, Popeye, who instilled the love of poetry and writing in his grandson.

LGP34 **September—A Walk in Hendricks Park (1994)**

Patrick Tilcock
Brush lettering by Marilyn Reaves

15 x 11 inches as a single sheet, folded to 7.5 x 5 inches

125 numbered copies signed by the author

Handset Perpetua types

Camel Hahnemühle Ingres paper

Attached on front of folded sheet is a small torn piece of Japanese bark paper

Presented in an envelope with a printed image of an aged leaf in which only the veins remain

LGP35 **Listening is a Very Deep Practice (2003)**

Thich Nhat Hanh

5.5 x 13 inches, single sheet

Undetermined edition size, no more than 50 copies

Handset Bembo types

Kitakata paper from Japan

Printed as a demonstration for a class I was teaching on broadside printing.

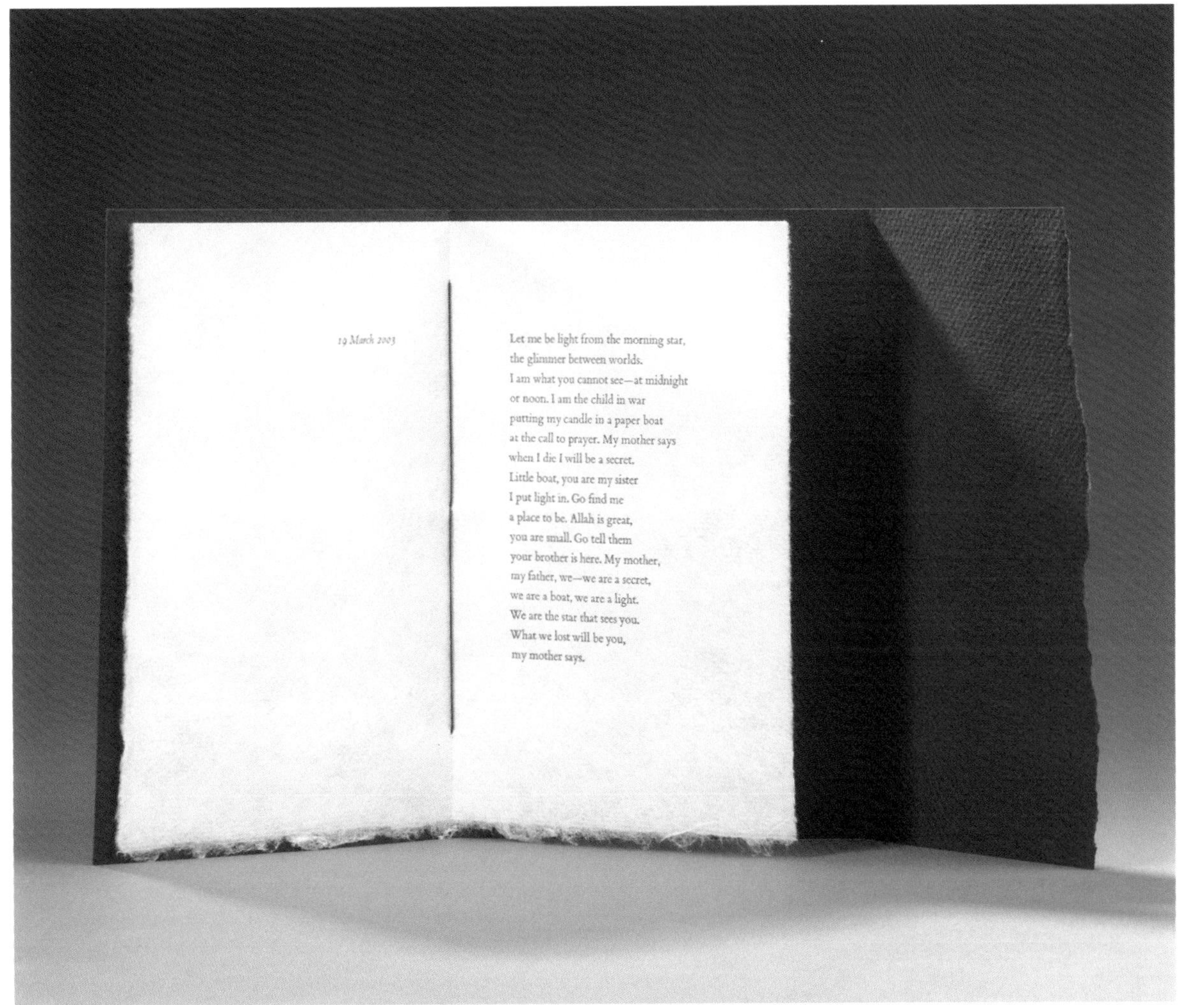
19 March 2003
Let me be light from the morning star,
the glimmer between worlds.
I am what you cannot see—at midnight
or noon. I am the child in war
putting my candle in a paper boat
at the call to prayer. My mother says
when I die I will be a secret.
Little boat, you are my sister
I put light in. Go find me
a place to be. Allah is great,
you are small. Go tell them
your brother is here. My mother,
my father, we—we are a secret,
we are a boat, we are a light.
We are the star that sees you.
What we lost will be you,
my mother says.

LGP36

LGP36 **A Prayer by the Tigris: 19 March 2003 (2003)**

Kim Stafford

Image on page 43

7.5 x 5 inches, 4 pages

220 numbered copies signed by the author

Handset Bembo types

Mulberry paper

Single folio pamphlet sewn to a paper tri-fold cover made of Canson Mi-Teintes

Right fold of cover sits on top and is torn; edge of tear colored using a silver Primacolor pencil

LGP37 **All Rights Reserved (2009)**

W. Patrick Tilcock

12 x 8.8 inches, single sheet

No more than 100 copies printed; a select few were signed

Handset Perpetua types

Nideggen paper

Printed at lone goose press with the assistance of guests at the press's annual Wayzgoose, November 1, 2009.

Weathergrams (2003 –)

Sandy and Patrick Tilcock

11 x 2.5 inches, top 2 inches folded over

Approximately 300 of each printed

Unnumbered and unsigned

The practice of "weathergrams" was developed by calligrapher and teacher Lloyd Reynolds in the early 1970s. It relates to a Japanese tradition of short informal poems exchanged among friends. A weathergram is a poem of ten words or less written on a strip of paper, then hung outdoors on a branch or bough to weather over a season, from solstice to equinox, or equinox to solstice. The poems are simple, spontaneous, and often refer to aspects of nature or the season.

A weathergram for each year is printed on different colored papers and with different typefaces or hand-lettering. Some include graphic designs or ornaments. They are given out at press functions and to friends in recognition of the friendship of the recipient.

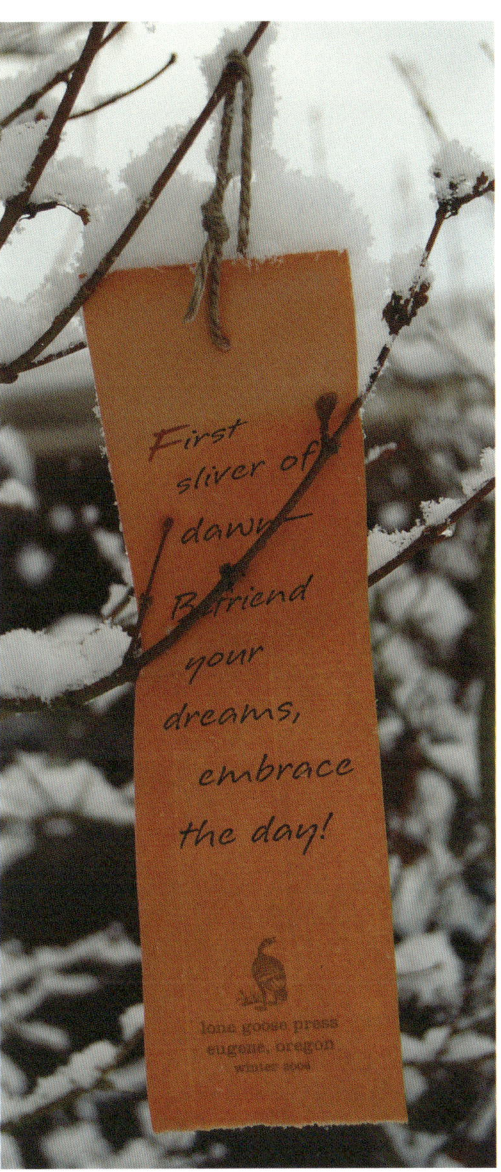

LGP41

LGP38 **The wind carries many messages** (Winter 2003)

LGP39 **Winter trees; bare branches reaching out & up in prayer** (Winter 2004)

LGP40 **Damp ruin of fallen leaves—Everywhere, bare stems hold next year's promise** (Winter 2005)

LGP41 **First sliver of dawn—Befriend your dreams, embrace the day!** (Winter 2006)

LGP42 **Clear water ripples over stone—Solitary heron guards the river's dreams** (Fall 2007)

LGP43 **Darting & hovering amid bursts of red—sipping summer wine** (Fall 2008)

LGP44 **Two hawks too high to hunt—Slow sky-dance** (Fall 2009)

LGP45 **The world forgotten, spinning with dragonflies.** (Fall 2010)

LGP46 **Great shaggy sunflower—summer's extravagant gift!** (Fall 2011)

LGP47 **Clear, crisp morning—river geese gossip among themselves!** (Spring 2012)

LGP48 **Mist clearing, tide withdrawing—are we on the beach or in the sky?** (Spring 2012)

LGP49 **Undulating chevron of geese chanting winter's approach** (Fall 2013)

“Readers respond directly to the emotional impact and aesthetic beauty of Sandy’s work.”

In the fall of 1985, Sandy Tilcock, an already accomplished bookbinder and box maker from Eugene, Oregon, enrolled in the newly established M.F.A. in the Book Arts program at the University of Alabama. She was looking forward to honing her skills and learning new binding techniques. Unfortunately the new binding instructor had very little to offer Sandy. As Sandy’s frustration with the binding program mounted, she became more and more involved in the printing projects assigned in the typographic laboratory. They offered her a means of being creative with text and type, incorporating the precise techniques that I taught my students.

The Book Arts program had two tracts: printing and binding. Students were required to major in one and minor in the other. In the spring of 1986, sitting in on one of my printing classes, Sandy printed “March: The Geese Return,” which is an excerpt from *A Sand County Almanac* by Aldo Leopold. Being a perfectionist in all that she undertakes, she found that printing could be very rewarding and that she could apply her sharp sense of craftsmanship and attention to detail that she had until then demonstrated only in her binding and box making. Another feature of this, and the next book, is the beautiful calligraphy by Edie Roberts. Sandy was to continue using calligraphy and brush lettering to great advantage in her future work.

The previous semester, Sandy had taken my course in basic typography, where she had to set all her projects using a single font of 16-point Van Dijck type. One of the goals of this course was to refine the typography by letter- and word-spacing the text. These two skills have distinguished all of Sandy’s later projects, including her imaginative broadsides.

So it came as no surprise to me when, in the spring of 1987, Sandy, together with another binding major, Rosalinda Gross-Smith, decided to design and print a book that they could bind as an edition binding. They undertook this as a directed study project through the Institute for the Book Arts, and I was their faculty advisor. The project was *Acknowledging the Presence of the Other* by Carolyn Servid, an exceedingly handsome book in an album format. It was printed on a Vandercook 219 press. All of Sandy’s subsequent work was printed on this type of press. They also made their own stunning paste papers to cover the boards of the edition.

After returning to Eugene, she established the lone goose press, a literary fine press, in 1989. Sandy was, from the very beginning, up to the challenge of producing finely crafted books. Even though her Vandercook press has a mechanized inking system, the actual presswork requires constant attention to pressure and inking. She has never been afraid to try new technologies. Many of her books are set by hand, but she is also amenable to using digitally set type, which she prints from polymer plates. For a forthcoming project, *All of Him* by Michael and Matthew Dickman, illustrated by Keith Achepohl, the original trace monotypes were scanned and then adjusted in Photoshop, after which photopolymer photogravure plates were made. They were then printed on a Takach etching press.

At a symposium on Sandy's work at the Jacobs Gallery in Eugene on May 30, 2012, Sandy said, "It's not about me," but I beg to differ with her. It is about her. She also said that the focus should always be on the text itself, the books themselves, not the printer. This is true, but without Sandy and her decisions these books would not have been printed. Her selection of texts is always personal and reflects a keen sense of community and a deep-rooted commitment to environmental issues. Her choices in text, typefaces, papers, and inks, as well as the binding, reflect her personality and interests. If someone else had printed these same texts, they would look very different. Readers respond directly to the emotional impact and aesthetic beauty of Sandy's work. When one sees an assortment of fine press books, it is usually easy to pick out the lone goose press books from the others.

— GABRIEL RUMMONDS

NOT ONLY THE PRINTER, BUT ALSO THE READER can feel the sensual experience of the book. When a handpress book is first opened, all of the reader's senses will instantly come alive. The hand responds to the tactility of the paper, the barely visible bite of the type in the paper; the eye is drawn to the richness of the ink impressed into the paper, the beauty of the illustrations; the nose picks up the smell of the size in the paper and the myriad scents of the binding materials; the ear acknowledges the crackle of the paper as the leaves are turned. And last, but by no means to be overlooked, the pleasure of reading the text in such a special format. The hand-printed book may have been created as an object, but it is after all, and will always remain, primarily a container for the author's words and ideas.

Richard-Gabriel Rummonds

Gabriel Rummonds

Excerpt from "Confessions of a Lapsed Handpress Printer;" Spring, 1997 issue of *The Book Club of California Quarterly News-Letter*. Wood engraving by Susan Lowdermilk. Printed by lone goose press for the University of Oregon Knight Library's Wayzgoose, October 22, 1998.

LGP61

LONE GOOSE PRESS COMMISSION WORK

LGP50 **For Calyx (1991)**

Ursula K. Le Guin
Linocut by Darryla Green-McGrath

21.6 x 10.1 inches, single sheet

75 numbered copies signed by the artist; copies 1–25 are also signed by the author

Handset Joanna types

Arches Text Wove paper

The poem was a gift from the author to Calyx at its 1989 Glitterati Soiree.

The press produced this broadside as a donation to Calyx, an independent press focused on nurturing women's creativity by publishing fine literature and art by women.

LGP51 **Tangerine Gifts: Travels in Tohuko, Japan, 1990 & 1991 (1992)**

David Grant Best and Brooks Jensen

11.4 x 13.8 inches, 12 pages

100 numbered copies signed by the artists

Handset Perpetua types

Arches Text Wove paper

Western calligraphy by Marilyn Reaves; Japanese calligraphy by Noboru Tarui; reproduced using magnesium plates

Sewn as a single signature and bound in boards covered with plum book cloth; front bears an impression of two tangerines and a label printed with a mahogany wood grain; title "Tangerine Gifts" appears in both Japanese and English characters

Each folio contains two photographs, one by each author, on the interior of each board; the edition has four different matched pairs of photographs

Commissioned by the authors.

This ambitious project proved to be more complex and expensive than the clients were prepared for. I designed and printed the pages and designed the binding before the project was cancelled. Only a few copies were completed as originally conceived.

LGP52 **Stepping Westward** (1992)

Sallie Tisdale
Woodcut by Susan Lowdermilk

Calligraphic initial by Edie Roberts reproduced using a magnesium plate

8.5 x 13.7 inches, single sheet

265 unnumbered copies; some were signed

Handset Perpetua type

Commercial paper made from recycled fibers

Some presented in a folder covered with green mohair book cloth and some presented in a paper folder

Excerpt from *Stepping Westward: The Long Search for Home in the Pacific Northwest,* Sallie Tisdale (Henry Holt, 1991)

Printed for the University of Portland, Portland, Oregon, to honor the occasion of the author's visit to the Arthur and Dorothy Schoenfeldt Distinguished Writers Series.

LGP53 **A Mountain Range Without Wolves (1993)**

Stephen Trimble

13.4 x 6.4 inches

Handset Perpetua types

Nideggen paper

Full sheet was 13.4 x 19.2 inches; top of sheet torn, hand-colored, and then folded to evoke a mountain landscape

160 unnumbered copies

Some presented in a folder covered in a natural linen book cloth

Excerpt from *The Sagebrush Ocean: A Natural History of the Great Basin*, Stephen Trimble (University of Nevada Press, 1989)

Printed for the University of Portland, Portland, Oregon, to honor the occasion of the author's visit to the Arthur and Dorothy Schoenfeldt Distinguished Writers Series.

LGP54 **Opus from Space (1994)**

Pattiann Rogers

13 x 7 inches, single sheet

Handset Perpetua types

Nideggen paper

Edition size unknown

This poem was later included in the author's *Eating Bread and Honey* (Milkweed Editions, 1997).

Printed for the University of Portland, Portland, Oregon, to honor the occasion of the author's visit to the Arthur and Dorothy Schoenfeldt Distinguished Writers Series.

LGP55 **To Develop the Youth (1996)**

Maude Kerns
Woodcut by Susan Lowdermilk

Calligraphic initial by Edie Roberts reproduced using a magnesium plate

14 x 9.8 inches, single sheet

50 numbered copies

Handset Perpetua type

Gray Rives BFK paper

Commissioned by Maude Kerns Art Center, Eugene, Oregon, to commemorate the first annual Maude Kerns Duchess Award.

LGP56 **To Be Afraid of What Is Different (1997)**

Maude Kerns
Woodcut by Susan Lowdermilk

Calligraphic initial by Edie Roberts reproduced using a magnesium plate

14 x 9.8 inches, single sheet

50 numbered copies

Handset Perpetua type

White Rives BFK paper

Commissioned by Maude Kerns Art Center, Eugene, Oregon, to commemorate the second annual Maude Kerns Duchess Award.

LGP57 **Apologia** (1997)

Barry Lopez
Woodcuts by Robin Eschner
Image on page 54

11.8 x 11 inches, 24 pages

50 numbered copies and 16 lettered copies for the participants and those who supported the publication, signed by the author and the artist

Computer-set Poppi Laudatio Regular and Trajan, printed using polymer plates

Stonehenge paper

Individual folios hinged together to form a more than 20-foot-long continuous image; bound in boards using Lama Li handmade paper and original USGS topographic maps of the State of Wyoming

Enclosed in a folder on the back cover, on an original USGS topographic map of Wyoming, is a tire-tread print made by Barry Lopez with the assistance of Sandy Tilcock, using the inked tire of Barry's Toyota 4-Runner, the vehicle driven on the journey from Oregon to Indiana that is chronicled in the essay

Housed in a clamshell box covered with black Canapetta book cloth, with a paper label on the spine

The twenty-three woodblocks were carved on poplar by Robin Eschner, of Forestville, California, over a period of six years. Charles Hobson, of San Francisco, designed and organized the edition, which was printed by Susan Acker at Feathered Serpent Press, Novato, California. The woodblocks were made into an edition by Nora Pauwels at the Kala Art Institute in Berkeley, California. John DeMerritt, of Emeryville, California, hinged the text pages and bound the book. Sandy Tilcock of lone goose press, Eugene, Oregon, produced the boxes.

This was an unusual project, in that I did not have responsibility for all the production work but oversaw those who did the work and published it under my imprint. It came about because the original publisher was unable to follow through due to illness. Robin was anxious to see the book completed and be included in a large exhibition based on Barry Lopez's writings scheduled at a gallery in San Francisco. Barry approached me and asked if I would become the publisher and shepherd the project to completion. We had only three months to produce the book, so no one person would be able to do all the work. It became a team approach. As the publisher, my role was to assure that everyone was on task so we could meet the deadline. Since we were hiring out much of the work, it was important to find funding. Barry and I worked together and solicited pre-publication subscribers. It was a crazy undertaking but we met the deadline and as a result I developed several good friends. I had daily conversations with both Charles Hobson and Robin Eschner. When the book was done I found myself missing those conversations as they embraced more than the book. Robin and I soon discovered a shared passion for the canine family, and my friendship with her continues today. I have also had the privilege to work with her since then. My relationship with Barry continues. Some project memories: my dog Ursula riding in the truck with Barry when he drove over the maps; Robin collapsing in laughter as I described over the phone "a little trouble with registration" while printing the tire treads.

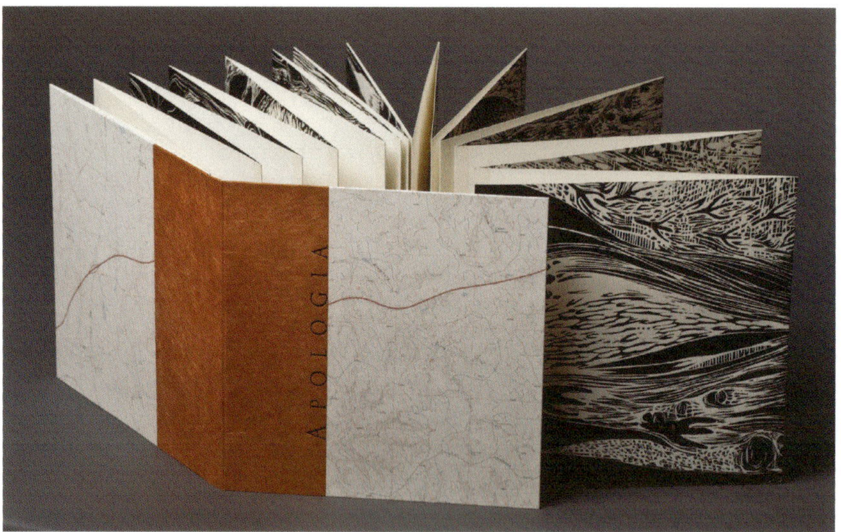

LGP57

LGP58 **Sagebrush: A Visual and Literary Homage to the Great Basin Desert (1997)**

Natalie Sudman
Images and collage by Terri Warpinski

10.8 x 8.9 inches, 16 pages

50 numbered copies and 10 lettered copies for participants, signed by the author and the artist

Computer-set Perpetua type for the text and Charlemagne type for the display, printed using polymer plates

Line drawings reproduced using magnesium plates

Gray Rives BFK paper

Single signature sewn into a four-panel folded case with brown Iris book cloth over boards; inside back cover is an original collage of photos and printed images with a covered mat surrounding the collage

Commissioned by Natalie Sudman and Terri Warpinski, this piece was the result of a collaborative design between the artists and SandyTilcock.

LGP59 **Dogwood (1997)** Dogwood Editions

Portfolio of eight drypoint images by Barbara Bartholomew (1), Frank Boyden (1), C. T. Feathers (1), T. W. Kearcher (3), Sandra Lopez (1) and R. C. Pickering (1)

14.1 x 11.4 inches, 11 unbound sheets

10 copies numbered and signed by the artists

Computer-set Baskerville types for supporting material printed using polymer plates

Drypoints printed by Martha Pfanschmidt and Tom Prochaska of Atelier Mars Press, Portland, Oregon

Housed in a clamshell box covered with a natural linen book cloth

The portfolio is in memory of Toni, T. W. Kearcher's dog, whom all involved in this project dearly loved.

Commissioned by T. W. Kearcher.

LGP60 **Hendricks Park (1997)**

Neill Archer Roan
Cobweb drawing by Anne Korn
Brush lettering by Marilyn Reaves reproduced using a magnesium plate

8.5 x 6.8 inches, single sheet

55 numbered copies and signed by the author

Handset Perpetua types

Gray Rives BFK paper

Cobweb reproduced using magnesium plates, printed with white ink, then dusted with a pearlescent silver dry pigment

Commissioned by the author.

LGP61 **Not Only the Printer (1998)**

Richard-Gabriel Rummonds
Wood engraving by Susan Lowdermilk
Image on page 48

13 x 5.3 inches, single sheet

250 unnumbered copies signed by the author

Handset Perpetua types

Cream Zerkall book paper

Presented in a sealed paper sleeve

Excerpt from "Confessions of a Lapsed Handpress Printer," Richard-Gabriel Rummonds (The Book Club of California Quarterly, spring, 1997)

Commissioned by the University of Oregon Knight Library for it's October 22, 1998 Wayzgoose.

LGP62 **Prayer (1999)**

Tom Crawford
Drawing by Adrian Arleo reproduced using a magnesium plate

16 x 8 inches, single sheet

100 numbered copies signed by the author

Handset Centaur types

Nideggen paper

Commissioned by the poet.

LGP63 **Wild Mercy (2003)**

Terry Tempest Williams
Brush lettering by Marilyn Reaves reproduced using a magnesium plate

7.2 x 14.8 inches, single sheet

250 unnumbered copies, some signed by the author

Handset Centaur type

Nideggen paper

Excerpt from *Red Passion and Patience in the Desert,*
Terry Tempest Williams (Pantheon Books, 2001)

Printed as a gift for the Castle Rock Collaboration and
Utah Open Lands.

Commissioned by the author.

LGP64 **We Regard Ourselves as Servants of Memory (2005)**

Barry Lopez
Image on page 58

6.3 x 7.7 inches, 4 pages

150 numbered copies signed by the author

Handset Gill Sans types

Earth Zerkall Ingres paper

French fold sewn into a grigio Fabriano Ingres paper cover

Logo for BRING Recycling, Lane County, Oregon, printed on front cover

Excerpt from "Apocalypse," which appears in *Resistance*, Barry Lopez (Knopf, 2004)

This was a gift for those who attended "Rejuvenate," a benefit held on March 31, 2005, for BRING Recycling of Lane County, Oregon, with featured speaker Barry Lopez.

Commissioned by BRING Recycling.

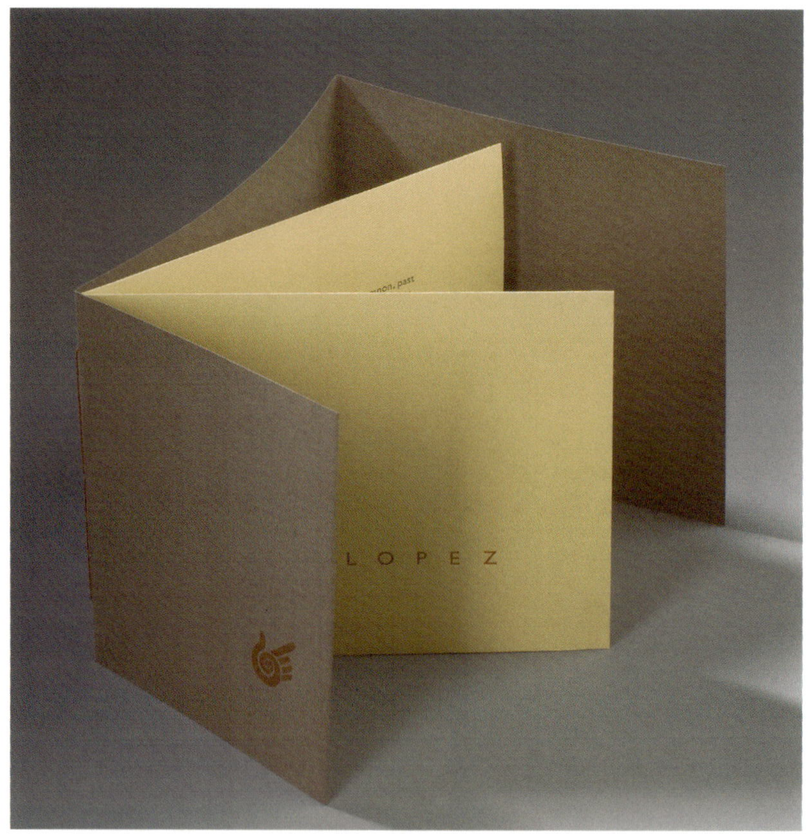

LGP64

LGP65 **Grandfather Was a Good Witch: Growing Up Cherokee** (2006)

Rennard Strickland and Jack Gregory
Illustrations by Margot Voorhies Thompson reproduced using polymer plates
Image on page 60

10 x 8.4 inches, 36 pages

101 numbered copies and 10 lettered copies for participants, signed by the authors and the artist

Michael Bixler's monotype-cast Gill Sans type, then passed through the composing stick for justification; computer-set Neuland for the display type and printed using polymer plates

Nideggen paper

Sewn binding with a supported paper wrapper made from a handmade pigmented and dyed flax paper (Walnut Red) by Cave Papers

Original images cut large in Rubylith film and reproduced to size using polymer plates

Commissioned by Rennard Strickland.

One of my favorite commissions. Rennard Strickland was retiring from teaching and being Dean at the School of Law, University of Oregon. He was marking the end of forty years of teaching and wished to publish his fortieth book in conjunction with his retirement. He commissioned me to do this and I gladly accepted the challenge.

The story grew from what Rennard writes "may be our greatest literary failure." After the publication of Strickland's and Gregory's first book, *Sam Houston with the Cherokees, 1829–1833,* (University of Texas Press, 1967), they received a phone call from an editor at Random House asking if they would do a "children's book on what it's like to be an Indian."

They agreed to undertake the task and took a tape recorder out into the field to gather impressions and experiences. They interviewed more than two dozen Cherokee men who had come of age during the Great Depression. Reels and reels of tape and dozens of letters later, the New York editor decided Strickland's and Gregory's Indians did not meet her stereotype of what it was like to be Indian. By mutual agreement, the project was called off.

Strickland and Gregory gathered those stories into one narrative which was published in 1972 as *Adventures of an Indian Boy* by the Indian Heritage Association. *Grandfather Was a Good Witch* is a slightly different version of the 1972 publication.

Rennard enjoys the whole process of making a book, from writing to fine-tuning the text, selecting papers (he loved "fondling" paper), typeface, images, etc. He is an absolute joy to work with.

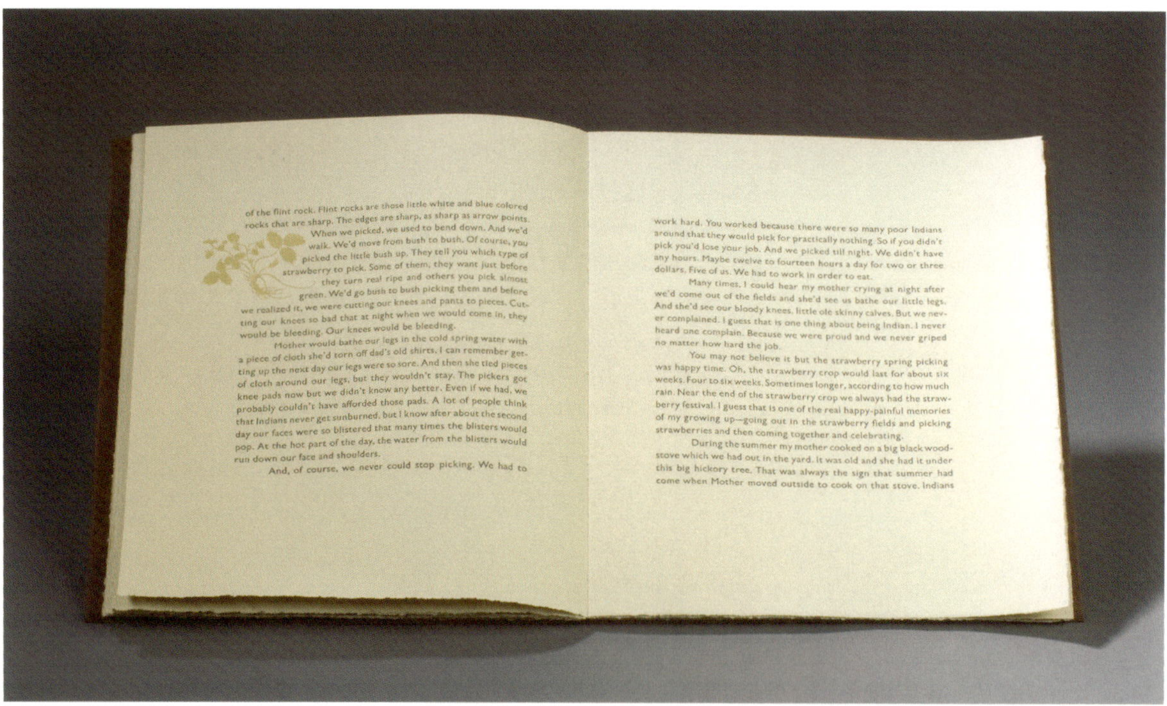

of the flint rock. Flint rocks are those little white and blue colored rocks that are sharp. The edges are sharp, as sharp as arrow points.

When we picked, we used to bend down. And we'd walk. We'd move from bush to bush. Of course, you picked the little bush up. They tell you which type of strawberry to pick. Some of them, they want just before they turn real ripe and others you pick almost green. We'd go bush to bush picking them and before we realized it, we were cutting our knees and pants to pieces. Cutting our knees so bad that at night when we would come in, they would be bleeding. Our knees would be bleeding.

Mother would bathe our legs in the cold spring water with a piece of cloth she'd torn off dad's old shirts. I can remember getting up the next day our legs were so sore. And then she tied pieces of cloth around our legs, but they wouldn't stay. The pickers got knee pads now but we didn't know any better. Even if we had, we probably couldn't have afforded those pads. A lot of people think that Indians never get sunburned, but I know after about the second day our faces were so blistered that many times the blisters would pop. At the hot part of the day, the water from the blisters would run down our face and shoulders.

And, of course, we never could stop picking. We had to work hard. You worked because there were so many poor Indians around that they would pick for practically nothing. So if you didn't pick you'd lose your job. And we picked till night. We didn't have any hours. Maybe twelve to fourteen hours a day for two or three dollars. Five of us. We had to work in order to eat.

Many times, I could hear my mother crying at night after we'd come out of the fields and she'd see us bathe our little legs. And she'd see our bloody knees, little ole skinny calves. But we never complained. I guess that is one thing about being Indian. I never heard one complain. Because we were proud and we never griped no matter how hard the job.

You may not believe it but the strawberry spring picking was happy time. Oh, the strawberry crop would last for about six weeks. Four to six weeks. Sometimes longer, according to how much rain. Near the end of the strawberry crop we always had the strawberry festival. I guess that is one of the real happy-painful memories of my growing up—going out in the strawberry fields and picking strawberries and then coming together and celebrating.

During the summer my mother cooked on a big black woodstove which we had out in the yard. It was old and she had it under this big hickory tree. That was always the sign that summer had come when Mother moved outside to cook on that stove. Indians

LGP65

LGP66 **The Way It Is (2009)**

William Stafford
Handmade paper and thread drawing by Helen Hiebert

18 x 12 inches, single sheet

50 numbered copies

Computer-set Stone Sans types printed using polymer plates

Thread drawing uses an actual length of thread drawn between two layers of handmade translucent abaca paper

Commissioned by Helen Hiebert.

LGP67 **Blank Paper (2009)**

R.D. Sage
Brush graphic by Marilyn Reaves
Image on page 63

19 x 12.5 inches, single sheet

40 numbered copies and 12 lettered copies

Computer-set Dante type printed using polymer plates

Off-white Rives BFK paper

The numbered copies are part of a suite of broadsides that were sold in Portland, Oregon, to support the non-profit organization Write Around Portland. The goals of Write Around Portland are to provide high-quality writing workshops in safe, accessible, and respectful environments, to hold community readings to promote the exchange of stories, and to publish anthologies connecting writers and readers. The poem is by one of the workshop participants.

The lettered copies were printed for subscribers of lone goose press broadsides.

I was one of ten letterpress printers asked to donate our services in this fund-raising project. We were given several selections of writings from workshop participants and asked to select one, then design and print a broadside using that text. The size of the broadside was specified; otherwise, any possibility was open.

LGP68 **The Two-Headed Calf (2013)**

Laura Gilpin
Graphic by Sandy Tilcock

15 x 11 inches, single sheet

Computer-set Optima and Beata types printed using polymer plates

Canal paper (Black Denim) from Saint-Armand paper mill in Montreal, Canada, made using a variety of recycled fibers

Starry night graphic based on a NASA photo found on the internet and reproduced using a polymer plate which was printed twice, shifting the plate horizontally and vertically about an inch for second printing; printed in white ink then hand-colored using a silver Prismacolor pencil

Poem appears in *The Hocus-Pocus of the Universe,* Laura Gilpin (Doubleday, 1977)

Commissioned by Jeremy Nissel to honor his partner Linda Ellis as she embarked upon her 61st revolution around the sun.

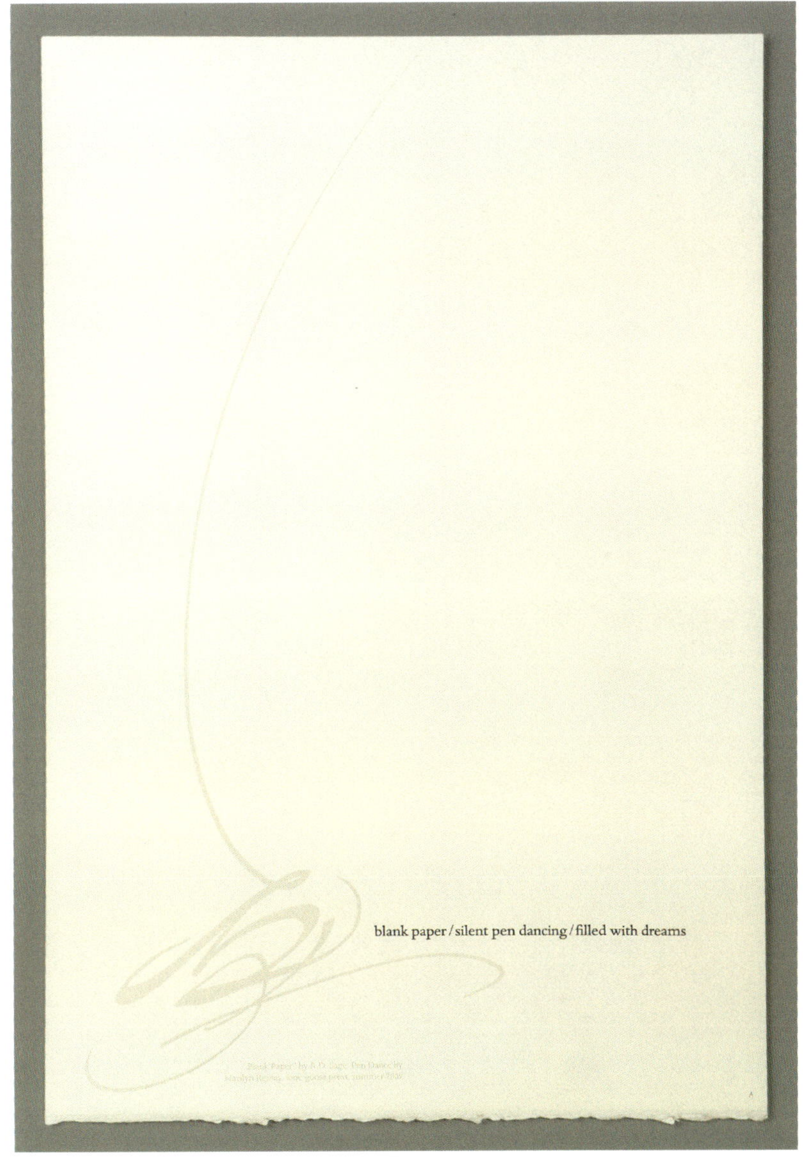

LGP67

Knight Library Press 1999–2006

In the summer of 1997, Bernie McTigue, then Director of Special Collections and Archives at the University of Oregon, approached me with an offer to start and head up a fine press within the University of Oregon Library. At first I was hesitant but then realized it was a great opportunity to share what I had started at lone goose press, and to teach classes and work with various departments on campus. It took over a year for George Shipman, then the University Librarian, to raise the monies necessary to take on such an endeavor. It was an interesting relationship, more of a public/private partnership. lone goose press would remain in its studio and the Library would lease the equipment; I would be a member of the Library Faculty and would continue to operate lone goose press as time permitted.

My duties included conceiving of and producing limited-edition, letterpress books and broadsides. The writers would be contemporary and we would commission original artwork. I also did custom binding and boxes for the Special Collections, taught workshops and classes in the Department of Art, and provided opportunities for the Library to showcase its collection and endeavors.

It was an incredible opportunity and I had the privilege of doing some amazing work while forging relationships with writers and artists and promoting the book arts.

Although Knight Library Press eventually had to close due to budget constraints, I will always be grateful for the opportunity to develop Knight Library Press and am proud of the work I did for the University.

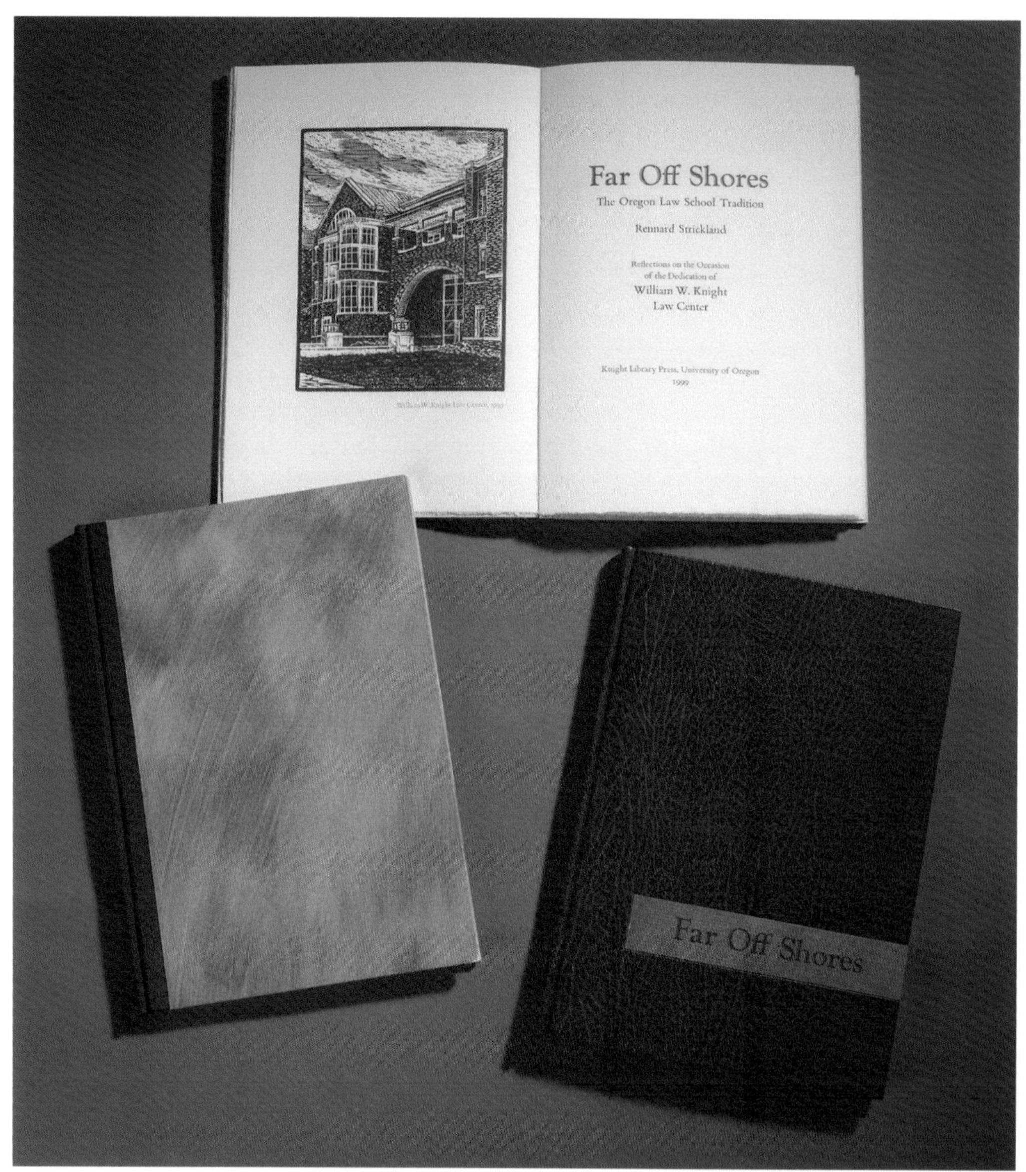
Far Off Shores
The Oregon Law School Tradition
Rennard Strickland
Reflections on the Occasion
of the Dedication of
William W. Knight
Law Center
Knight Library Press, University of Oregon
1999
Far Off Shores

KLP1

KLP1 **Far Off Shores: The Oregon Law School Tradition: Reflections on the Occasion of the Dedication of William W. Knight Law Center (1999)**

Rennard Strickland
Wood engravings by Susan Lowdermilk
Image on page 66

8.2 x 5.7 inches, 24 pages

150 numbered copies and 10 lettered participant copies signed by the author and the artist

Michael Bixler's monotype-cast Bembo type, then passed through the composing stick for justification; handset Goudy Hand tooled for the titling and opening initial

Hahnemüle Bugra paper

Paste papers for the covers designed by Sandy Tilcock and Judith Sparks; edition produced by Judith Sparks; stimulus for the paper design came from the slate floor of the Law Center

Books presented in four binding styles: 1–10 in full leather; 11–35 in cloth with paste paper over boards with paper label (short title) on spine; 36–60 in the style of Gary Frost's sewn board binding; and 61–150 in soft cover pamphlet with short title and author label on cover

This was the first major project for Knight Library Press. Rennard Strickland, then Dean of the Law School, was an enthusiastic advocate of the establishment of Knight Library Press. To show his support and belief in the need of Knight Library Press he asked it to produce this commemorative book to honor the dedication of the new law center. One of the full leather bindings was given to then Supreme Court Justice Sandra Day O'Connor who was the featured speaker at the building's dedication.

In the back of the book is written: "This publication was underwritten by an anonymous donor to honor Jane Gordon and Jane Gary whose dedication and determination ensured the completion of William W. Knight Law Center." Only after the project was done did I learn that Rennard Strickland was the anonymous donor.

"For the last fifteen years . . . Sandy Tilcock has been my muse . . ."

I suspect that of my fellow Cub Scouts in Den 8, Pack 12 at the Longfellow Grade School in Muskogee, Oklahoma, that I may be the only one who recalls that cold January day in 1948 when we called on the famous historian Grant Foreman. And I certainly do not expect that the Foreman Library, in which we were seated for the great man's lecture, to have been such a transformative experience for the others. It was at that very moment when his wife, also a famous historian, Carolyn Thomas Foreman, escorted a bunch of third and fourth graders into his book-lined study and library that I came upon my vocation in the form of "The Book". And I must say that I never regretted my subsequent devotion to the book arts.

Many years later, while I was in law school at the University of Virginia in Charlottesville when I became so bored with my legal studies, I began writing my first book, entitled *Sam Houston with the Cherokees*. When I came home to Muskogee after my first year in Charlottesville, Jack Gregory and I went once again to see by now the widow of Grant Foreman, who was that summer turning ninety-eight. Despite the fact that it was an Oklahoma heat wave outside, I couldn't help but remember that cold January day back in 1948 when I had first made that trek.

Since that time, I have authored, co-authored, edited, co-edited any number of books. Many of these are limited editions, ranging from *Cherokee Spirit Tales* to *Grandfather Was a Good Witch*. And in addition to these volumes I have issued broadsides and other statements.

For the last fifteen years or so, Sandy Tilcock has been my muse—always ready with her book arts and letter press. Could you ask anything more of a good witch? Thank you, Sandy!

And what do I mean by the suggestion that Sandy Tilcock became my muse? I mean that she directed my thoughts about the work about which we were cooperating. For example, on *Grandfather Was a Good Witch,* she encouraged me to revise a little book which Jack Gregory and I had earlier published as *Adventures of an Indian Boy* and add the illustrations. The book took on a new life and became an interesting and much more complex book under the new title and with the new illustrations. We issued it as an independent lone goose press title in an edition of 101 copies.

— RENNARD STRICKLAND

KLP2 The Letters of Heaven (2000)

Barry Lopez
Five hand-colored etchings by Robin Eschner
Image on page 70

13.1 x 8.6 inches, 32 pages

125 numbered copies and 10 lettered participant copies signed by the author and artist

Calligraphic title, headings, and ornaments by Marilyn Reaves reproduced using polymer plates

Michael Bixler's monotype-cast Bembo type, then passed through the composing stick for justification

Hahnemühle Heine paper

Bound into a tri-fold cover made by laminating two handmade papers: Moulin de Larroque's Brown and Twinrocker's Mica Rose; title on cover of binding; a leather tie surrounds the cover

Short story from *Light Action in the Caribbean,* Barry Lopez (Knopf, 2000)

Selected by the Rounce & Coffin Club judges for inclusion in the 2001 Western Books Exhibition.

This was the first major publication of Knight Library Press and was dedicated to Ann and Fay Thompson who, through their generosity, helped make Knight Library Press a reality.

A special thanks was made to University Librarian George W. Shipman, who dared to imagine that Knight Library could embrace a fine press publishing program.

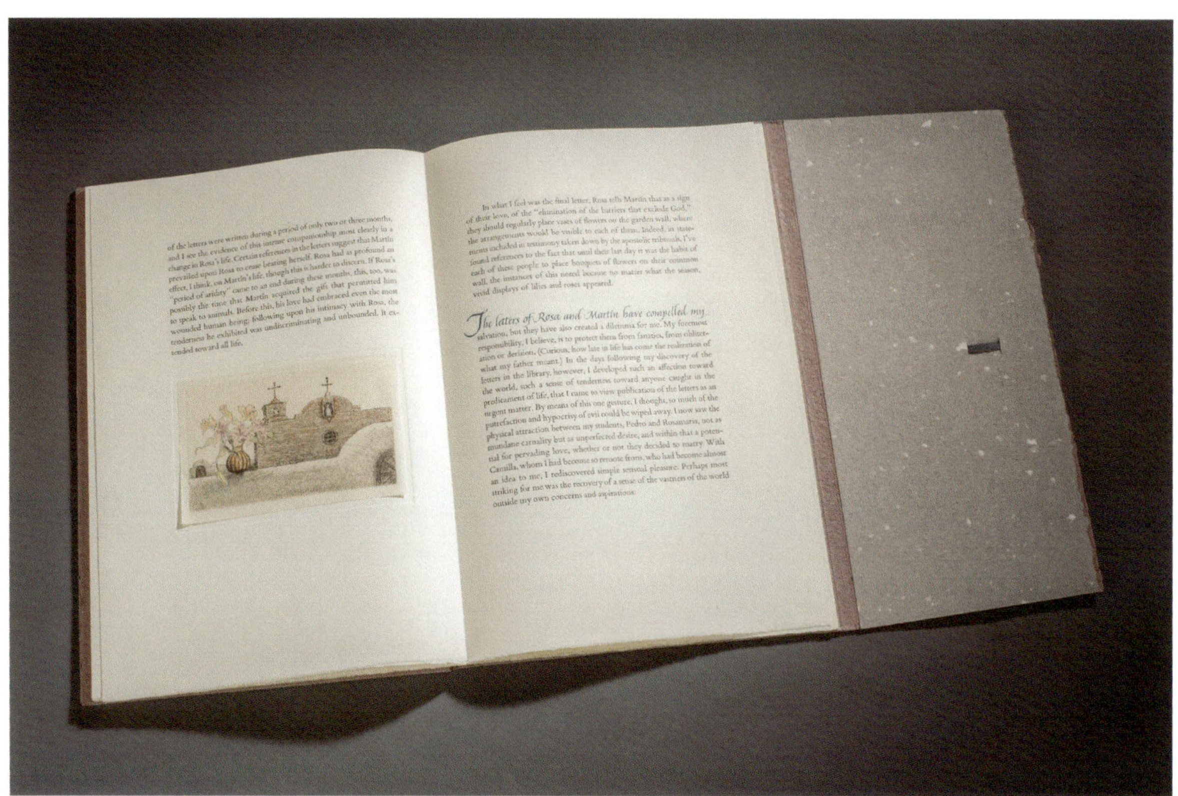

KLP2

KLP3 **Oregon Pilgrimage in Green: A Forest Journal for My Brother (2000)**

Kim Stafford

Drawings by Margot Voorhies Thompson reproduced using magnesium plates

6.4 x 12.1 inches, 18 pages

100 numbered copies and 10 lettered copies for participants, signed by the author and artist

Michael Bixler's monotype-cast Centaur and Arrighi types, then passed through the composing stick

Somerset Heavyweight book paper

Bound in boards in an accordion format (leporello) using earth Zerkall Ingres as the backing paper

An etching of a maidenhair fern printed on Kitikata green paper wraps around the cover boards

The book cascades, revealing a continuous image and text over 10 feet in length.

Awarded first place in fine press at the October 2002 Northwest Book Fest Book Arts Exhibition, a juried show of artists' and fine press books.

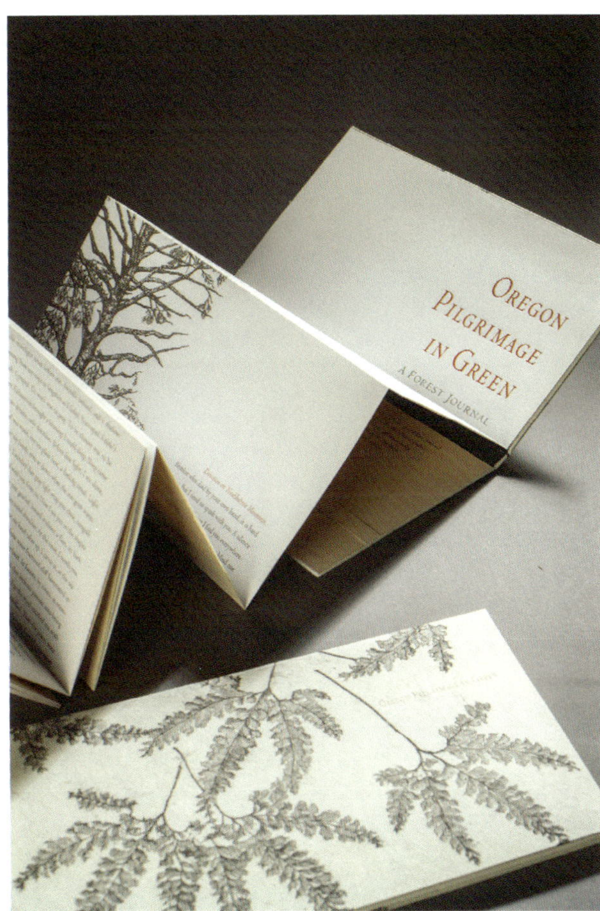

KLP3

A book that was a true collaboration from start to finish. I contacted Kim Stafford and Margot Voorhies Thompson to ask if they would be interested in collaborating on a book, doing something previously unpublished. We met and, after considerable discussion, selected a theme we wanted to pursue—looking at "place" as a source of healing—and a plan.

Kim would begin by writing. After a short period he sent us a draft. Margot and I were anticipating a poem, but it turned out to be more of a prose poem. We responded with our thoughts and Kim continued to edit and tighten his writing, continuing to ask for our feedback. After the fourth draft or so Margot and I began to see a direction we wanted this book to take. The text was about Kim's brother, Brett, and his death by suicide. Kim and Brett shared the landscape of Oregon while growing up, so Margot focused on drawing images of the Oregon landscape. I saw the book in an accordion format, running vertically to suggest going down deeper into the understory to make sense of the loss and to heal. From there it was a matter of evolution as the book, imagery, and text took shape, responding to each other.

All three of us are strong personalities so, predictably, there were times of conflict as to how to proceed. But we were all able to check our personal passions for the whole of the book, listening and responding to each other. I often referred to "taking our egos off and leaving them at the door" as one does with their shoes (which we did frequently when we met at Margot's shoe-free house).

At the public presentations and readings of the book we found that the discussion often turned to the topic of suicide and ways to make sense and heal from the trauma. We found it was a topic that has touched almost everyone and that we often do not have a way of talking about feelings related to this issue due to the taboo nature of the subject. This book gave people permission to do so. It is not often one gets to participate in such a project and I am honored that I was entrusted with this project.

KLP4 **Animals and People: The Human Heart in Conflict with Itself** (2002)

Pattiann Rogers
Etchings and illustrations by Margot Voorhies Thompson
Image on page 74

10.4 x 9.1 inches, 36 pages

100 numbered copies and 10 lettered copies for participants, signed by the author and the artist

Handset Bembo types for the text, computer-set Charlemagne for the title, printed using polymer plates

Hahnemühle Heine paper with the etchings printed on Sekishu mulberry paper

Etchings attached to text block by hinging the paper at both spine and foredge

Animal figures serving as page numbers originally cut from Rubylith film and reproduced to size using polymer plates

Bound in the style of Gary Frost's sewn-board binding with green goatskin leather on spine and paste papers designed and editioned by Sandy Tilcock over boards

Housed in a clamshell box covered in red mohair book cloth; bottom tray has a mat-like opening which holds a CD of Pattiann Rogers reading the poem which is protected by a wrapper made from the same edition of paste papers as used for cover

Until this book I had never printed an intaglio print. Accordingly, I hired an intaglio printer who specialized in edition printing to tutor me in the process. After all, I knew about ink and its properties and what the image should look like. What I learned was how to reproduce what the artist wanted. I was not interpreting the image. Margot commented: "Only you would take that on!" I like expanding my skill set!

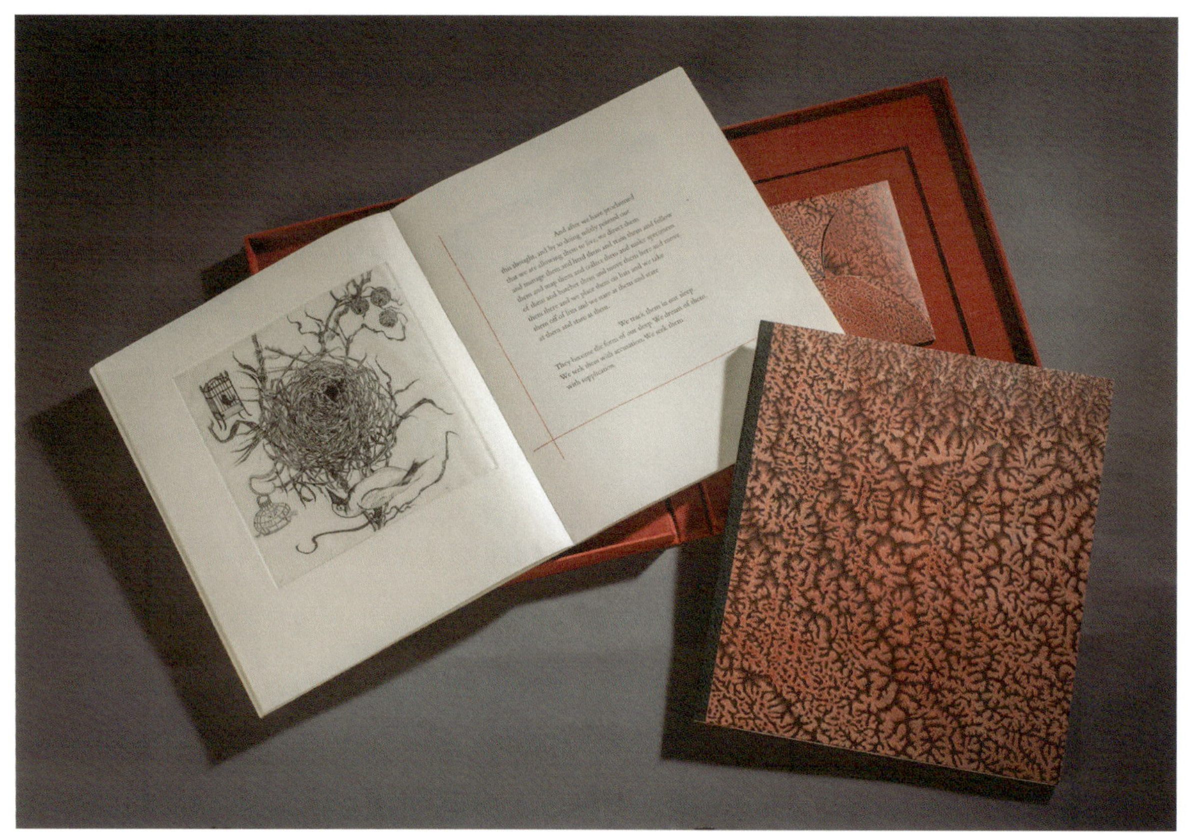

KLP4

KLP5 **Under the Oaks at Holmes Hall, Overtaken by Rain (1999)**

Garrett Hongo
Brush stroke by Marilyn Reaves reproduced using a polymer plate

17.5 x 11.5 inches

100 numbered copies signed by the author and the artist

Handset Perpetua types

Twinrocker handmade Tatyana paper

KLP6 **Earth Verse (2000)**

Gary Snyder
Brush design by Marilyn Reaves
Image on page 76

12 x 12 inches

100 numbered copies signed by the author

Handset Centaur types

Handmade jute-fiber paper from India, printed damp

Title and author separated by small rectangle of metallic copper acrylic paint added by hand

Poem from *Mountains and Rivers Without End,* Gary Snyder, (Counterpoint Press, 1996)

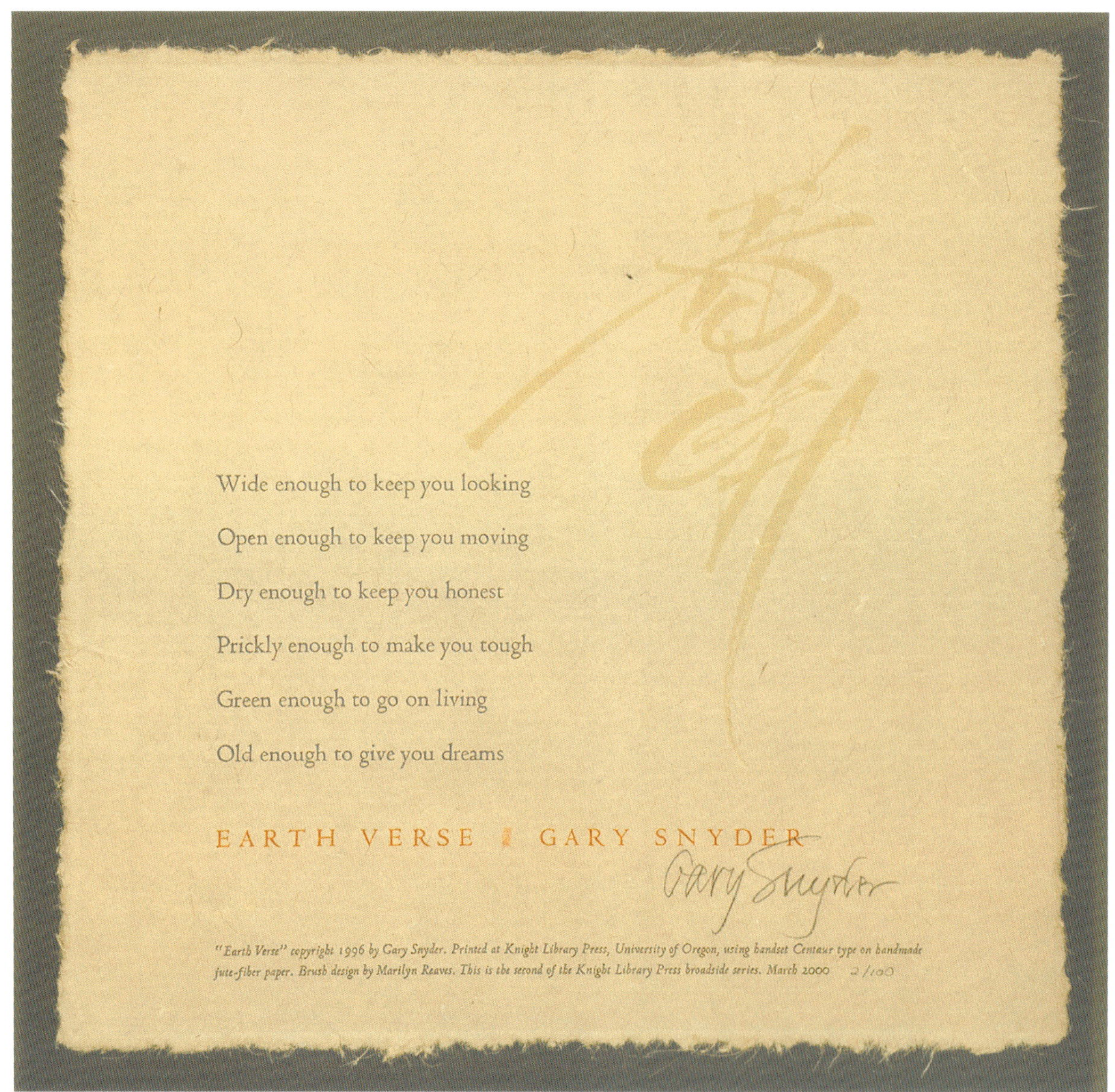
Wide enough to keep you looking
Open enough to keep you moving
Dry enough to keep you honest
Prickly enough to make you tough
Green enough to go on living
Old enough to give you dreams
EARTH VERSE GARY SNYDER
Gary Snyder
"Earth Verse" copyright 1996 by Gary Snyder. Printed at Knight Library Press, University of Oregon, using handset Centaur type on handmade jute-fiber paper. Brush design by Marilyn Reaves. This is the second of the Knight Library Press broadside series. March 2000 2/100

KLP6

KLP7 **Breath (2000)**

Wendell Berry
Woodcut by Margot Voorhies Thompson

16.5 x 10 inches

120 numbered copies signed by the author and the artist

Handset Centaur types

Sekishu paper from Japan

Woodcut printed on the back of the translucent paper

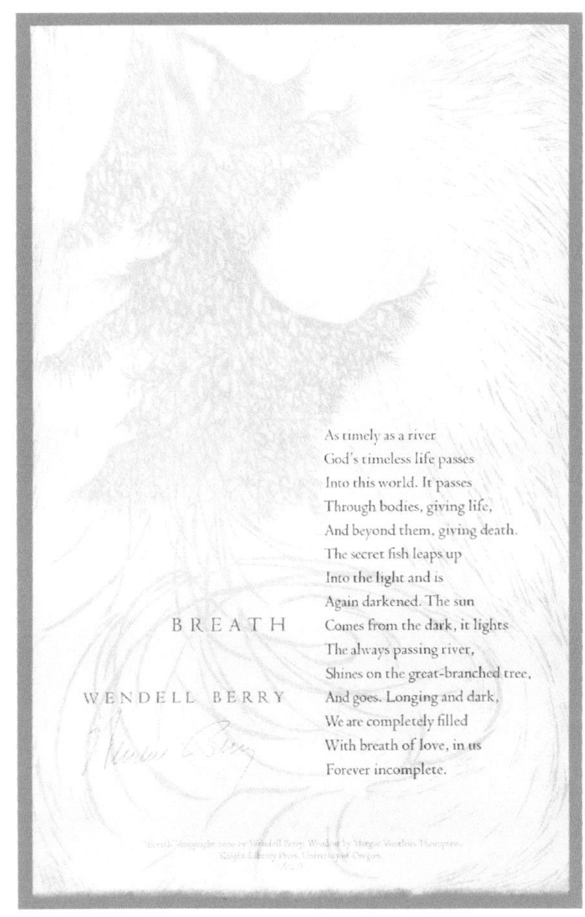

KLP7

KLP8 **Spirituality Is Solitary (2000)**

Terry Tempest Williams
Display lettering by Marilyn Reaves reproduced via polymer plates

11.5 x 19 inches

125 numbered copies signed by the author

Handset Centaur types

Twinrocker Simon's Green handmade paper

Presented in a tri-fold format of 11.5 x 6 inches inside a sleeve from Black Stonehenge paper; a circle is cut in front of sleeve which reveals the silver disk

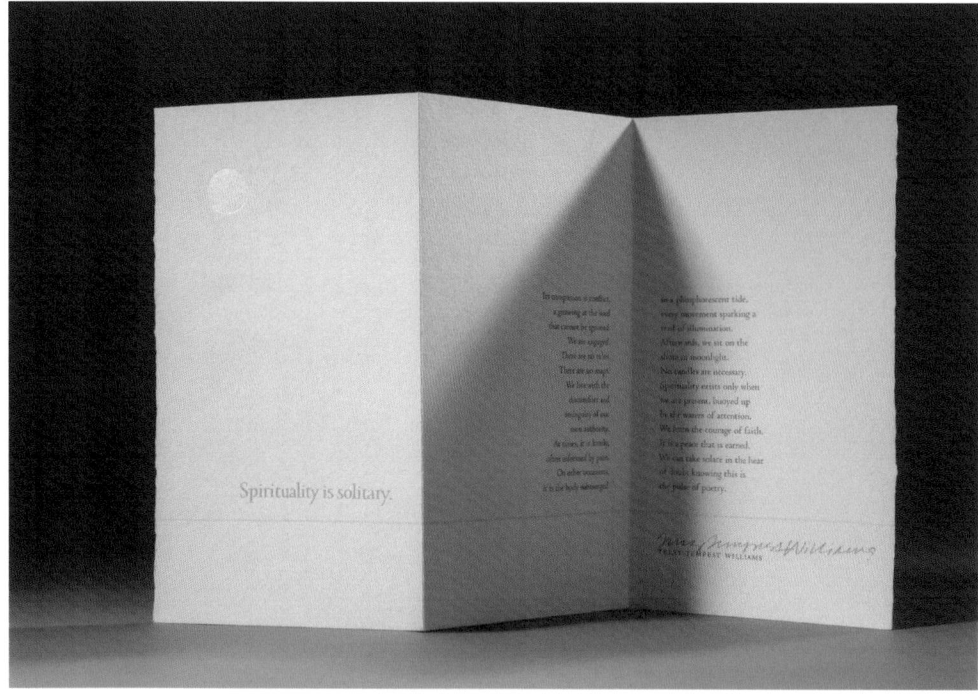

KLP8

KLP9 **There Is a Fire in the Water (2001)**

David James Duncan
Drawing by Frank Boyden reproduced using polymer plates
Image on page 80

18.5 x 11 inches

110 numbered copies signed by the author and the artist

Handset Perpetua types

Kitikata Green paper

Excerpt from *My Story as told by Water,* David James Duncan (Sierra Club Books, 2001)

I was setting the type for this broadside on September 11, 2001, while listening to the radio reports about the World Trade Center. The last lines of the text resonated with me at the time:

"There is a fire in water. There is an impossible flame, hidden in water, that creates not heat but life. Trusting the dying industrial river as we trust tomorrow's sunrise, possessing no other way, wild salmon climb entire mountain ranges in absolute earnest, solely to make contact with this flame."

My thought: Could we trust tomorrow's sunrise?

KLP10 **Read Then, If You Will (2001)**

John Daniel
Two-color woodcut by Susan Lowdermilk

19 x 10.5 inches

100 numbered copies signed by the author and the artist

Handset Perpetua types

Somerset Book paper

Fern Ridge Library, Veneta, Oregon commissioned this poem and it is included in an interior frieze.

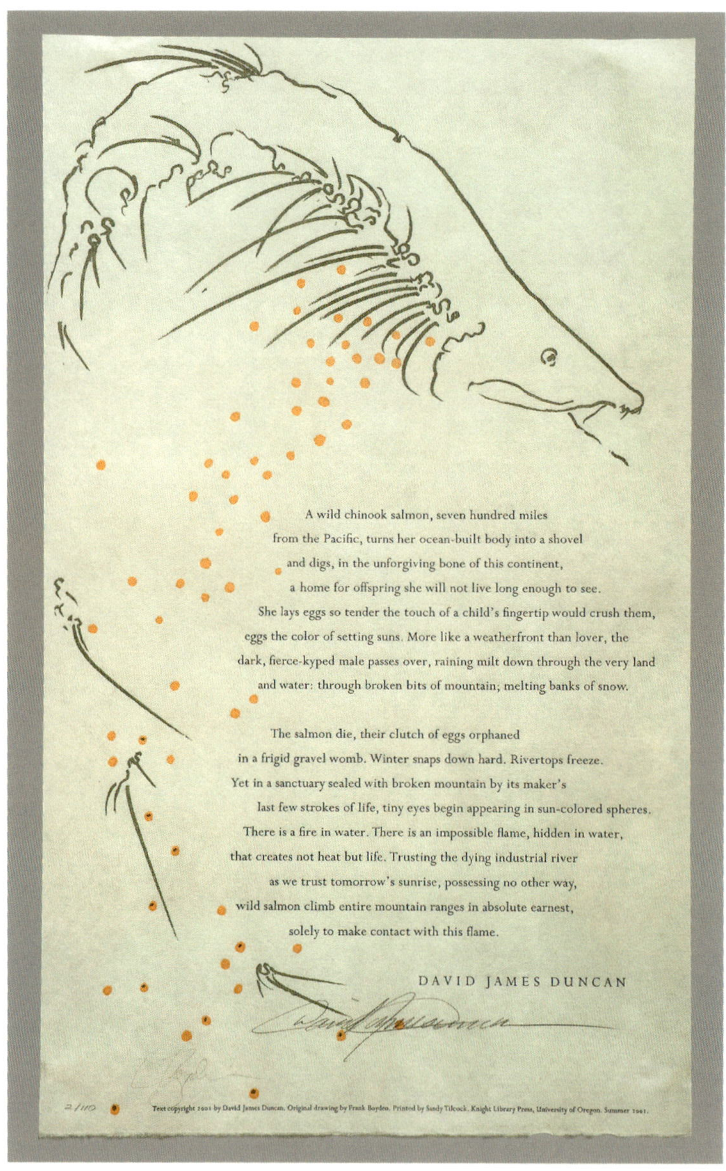

A wild chinook salmon, seven hundred miles
from the Pacific, turns her ocean-built body into a shovel
and digs, in the unforgiving bone of this continent,
a home for offspring she will not live long enough to see.
She lays eggs so tender the touch of a child's fingertip would crush them,
eggs the color of setting suns. More like a weatherfront than lover, the
dark, fierce-kyped male passes over, raining milt down through the very land
and water: through broken bits of mountain; melting banks of snow.

The salmon die, their clutch of eggs orphaned
in a frigid gravel womb. Winter snaps down hard. Rivertops freeze.
Yet in a sanctuary sealed with broken mountain by its maker's
last few strokes of life, tiny eyes begin appearing in sun-colored spheres.
There is a fire in water. There is an impossible flame, hidden in water,
that creates not heat but life. Trusting the dying industrial river
as we trust tomorrow's sunrise, possessing no other way,
wild salmon climb entire mountain ranges in absolute earnest,
solely to make contact with this flame.

DAVID JAMES DUNCAN

2/110

Text copyright 2001 by David James Duncan. Original drawing by Frank Boyden. Printed by Sandy Tilcock. Knight Library Press, University of Oregon. Summer 2001.

KLP9

KLP11 **The Circle of Life is Represented by the Osage Year (2001)**

Rennard Strickland
Relief engraving by Susan Lowdermilk

17 x 13.5 inches

80 numbered copies signed by the author and the artist

Handset Bembo types; computer-set Lithos type for titling, printed using polymer plates

Twinrocker handmade Cripple Creek paper, printed damp

Excerpt from *The Indians in Oklahoma,* Rennard Strickland (University of Oklahoma Press, 1980)

Commissioned by Rennard Strickland.

KLP12 **Kindness (2003)**

Naomi Shihab Nye
Image on page 82

25.3 x 7 inches

110 copies signed by the author

Handset Gill Sans type, computer-set Beata type for titling, printed using a polymer plate

Newsprint Somerset Velvet paper

Printed as a single sheet, backed with brick Hahnemüle Bugra, cut into seven panels and sewn as a Balinese binding that folds down to 3.6 x 7 inches

Presented in a black paper wrapper

Poem from *The Words Under the Words: Selected Poems,* Naomi Shihab Nye (Eighth Mountain Press, A Far Corner Book, 1995)

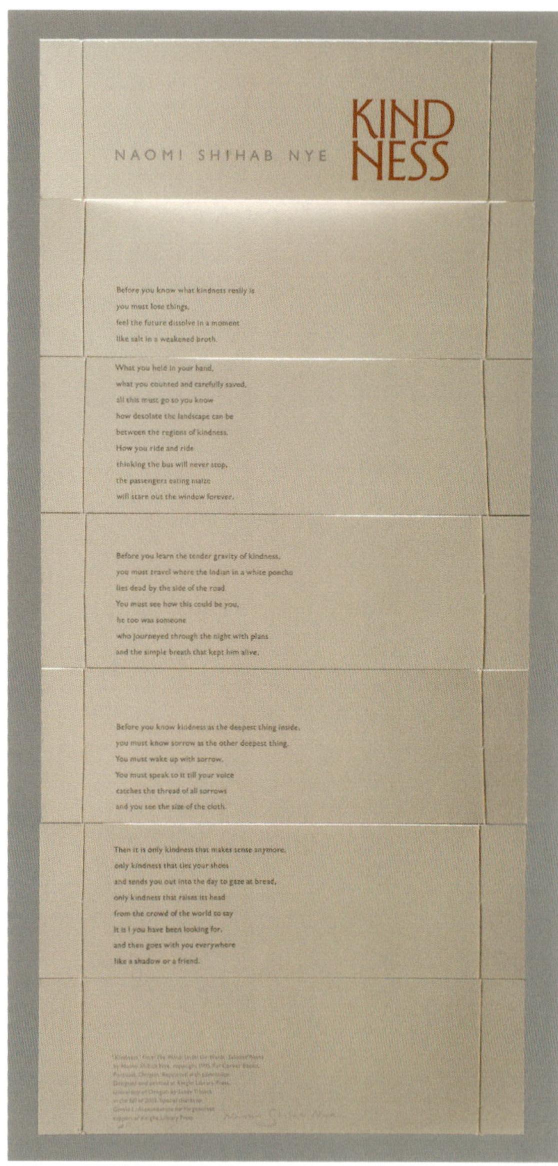
NAOMI SHIHAB NYE
KIND
NESS
Before you know what kindness really is
you must lose things,
feel the future dissolve in a moment
like salt in a weakened broth.
What you held in your hand,
what you counted and carefully saved,
all this must go so you know
how desolate the landscape can be
between the regions of kindness.
How you ride and ride
thinking the bus will never stop,
the passengers eating maize
will stare out the window forever.
Before you learn the tender gravity of kindness,
you must travel where the Indian in a white poncho
lies dead by the side of the road.
You must see how this could be you,
he too was someone
who journeyed through the night with plans
and the simple breath that kept him alive.
Before you know kindness as the deepest thing inside,
you must know sorrow as the other deepest thing.
You must wake up with sorrow.
You must speak to it till your voice
catches the thread of all sorrows
and you see the size of the cloth.
Then it is only kindness that makes sense anymore,
only kindness that ties your shoes
and sends you out into the day to gaze at bread,
only kindness that raises its head
from the crowd of the world to say
It is I you have been looking for,
and then goes with you everywhere
like a shadow or a friend.

KLP12

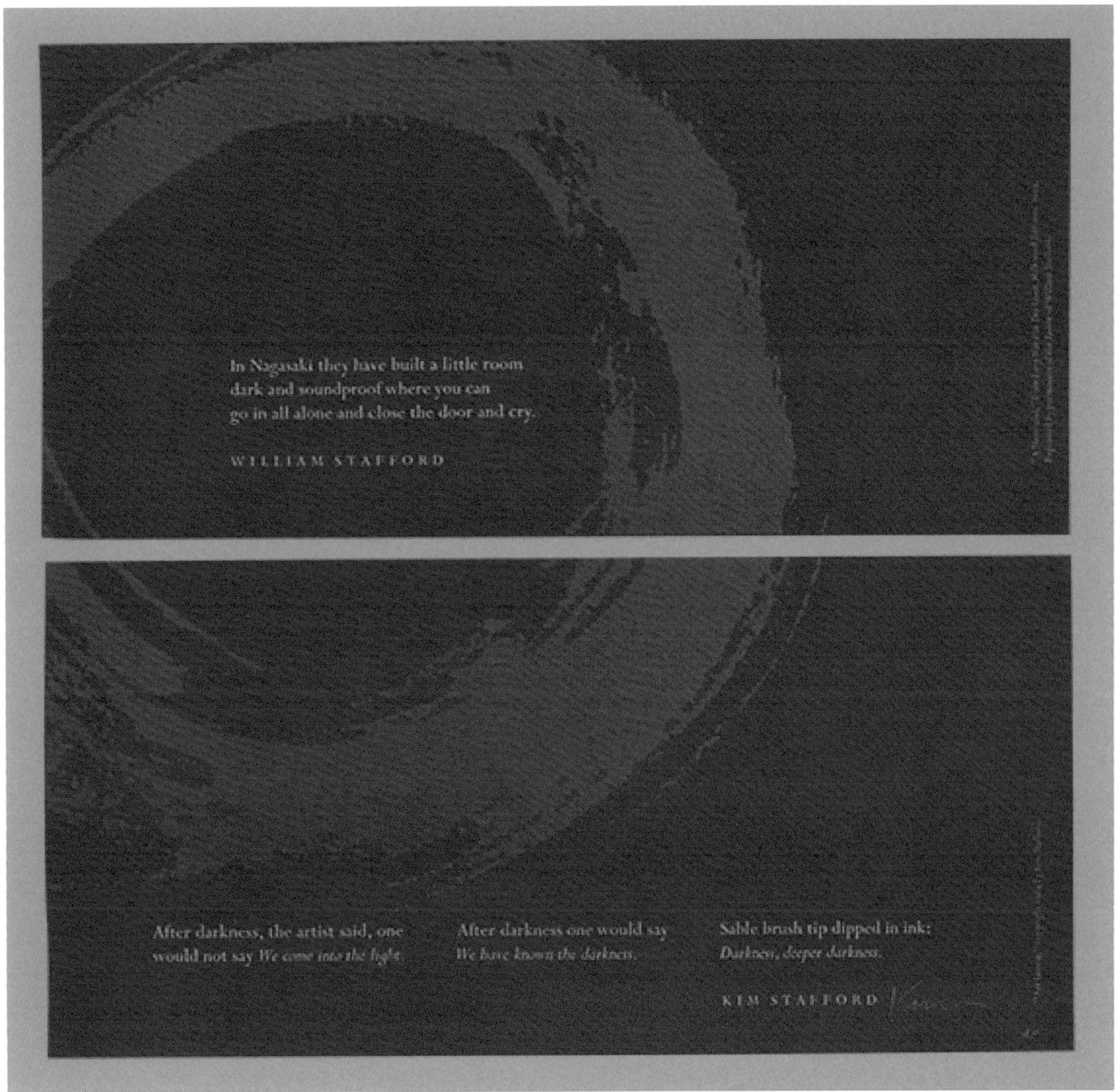
In Nagasaki they have built a little room
dark and soundproof where you can
go in all alone and close the door and cry.
WILLIAM STAFFORD
After darkness, the artist said, one
would not say We come into the light.
After darkness one would say
We have known the darkness.
Sable brush tip dipped in ink:
Darkness, deeper darkness.
KIM STAFFORD

KLP14

KLP13 **My Architect (2004)**

Sherman Alexie
Hand lettering for title by Marilyn Reaves and reproduced using a polymer plate

20.3 x 10.7 inches

115 numbered copies signed by the author

Handset Centaur types

Yatsuo paper from Japan consisting of Kozo fiber

KLP14 **A Memorial / Art Lesson (2004)**

William Stafford / Kim Stafford
Brush drawing of the enso by Marilyn Reaves reproduced using a polymer plate
Image on page 83

13 x 13 inches

85 numbered copies signed by Kim Stafford

Handset Perpetua types

Black Stonehenge paper printed damp

Printed as a single sheet, then cut in half to form a diptych that allows the two poems to stand separately or together (with a .5 inch separation in the center)

Kim Stafford and I collaborated on this broadside. Wishing to honor his father William's advocacy for peace, I selected three poems from *Every War has Two Losers* by William Stafford (Milkweed Editions, 2003). Kim then wrote companion poems for each of the three. I selected this pair to use for the broadside.

KLP15 **To Write . . . Is To Be Insane (2005)**

Molly Gloss

Original hand lettering by Marilyn Reaves reproduced using a polymer plate

16.5 x 7.3 inches

110 numbered copies signed by the author and the artist

Handset Bembo types

Mocha Hahnemühle Bugra paper

Hand lettering was dusted with autumn gold metallic dry pigment

Excerpt from *Wild Life: A Novel,* Molly Gloss (Simon & Schuster, 2000)

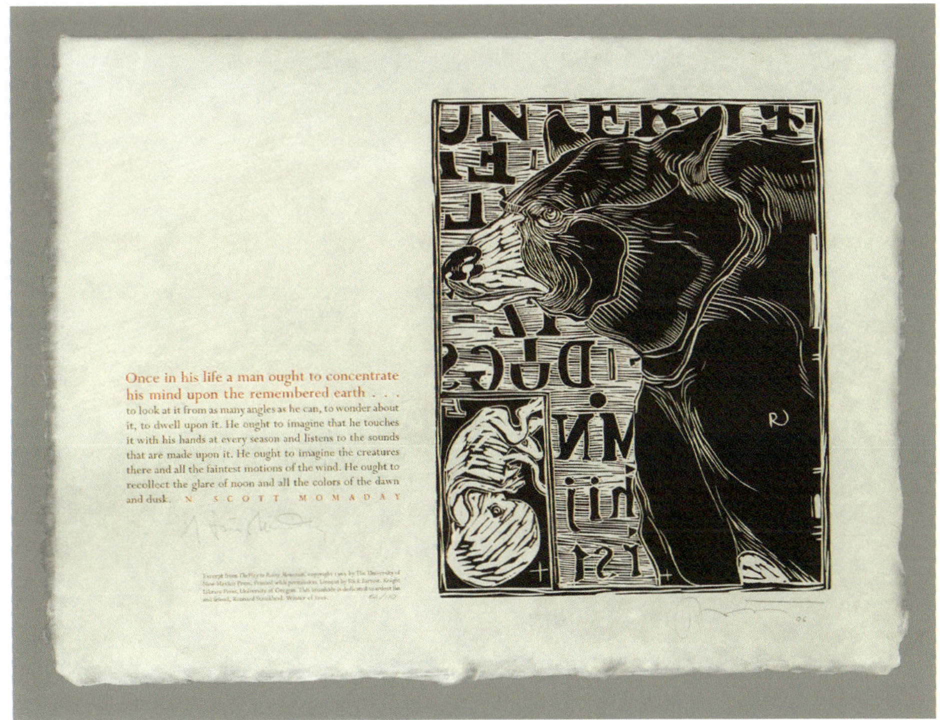

KLP16

KLP16 **Once in His Life (2006)**

N. Scott Momaday
Linocut by Rick Bartow
Image on page 85

12.8 x 17 inches

110 numbered copies signed by the author and the artist

Handset Perpetua types

Kitikata paper handmade in Japan

Excerpt from *The Way to Rainy Mountain,* N. Scott Momaday (University of New Mexico Press, 1969)

This broadside is dedicated to Rennard Strickland.

KLP17 **Design (2006)**

Billy Collins
Graphic by Sandy Tilcock reproduced using polymer plates

18 x 9 inches

102 numbered copies signed by the author

Handset Perpetua types, computer-set Copperplate 33bc for the display types and printed using polymer plates

Gray Mingei dyed paper from Japan

Printed in honor of the poet's visit to the University of Oregon, September 24, 2006.

The graphic, a circle, was done by sprinkling salt on the glass of the scanner, drawing a circle with my finger and then scanning the result. Enlarging the image provided the textured image which is printed white on the gray paper. Collins' poem begins:

> I pour a coating of salt on the table
> and make a circle in it with my finger.

"...the art of being unseen in the work."

The value of listing and describing the works of an artist often lies in the discovery of design elements and aesthetic choices that are common to some or all of the artist's works—and by implication point to the secrets of the artist's success. What then are we to make of this list and description of the first twenty-seven years of Sandy Tilcock's work as a fine press printer? A look at the descriptions of these pieces reveals no discernible pattern that would help us understand why we are so drawn to Sandy's work, or why we appreciate it beyond her choices of author and text, and of artist and image.

If we appreciate her work only for the language and ideas of the author and only for the accompanying images that invite us to read the text, Sandy will tell you that this is all she is striving for as a printer. Indeed, if the printing distracts the viewer from the text and image, it is defeating her aesthetic philosophy. The fine press printer is charged with creating a transparent window through which the viewer attends only to the scene beyond. Any smudge on the window is a distraction that threatens the artistic integrity of the piece. To Sandy, the proper role of the fine press printer—the essence of her aesthetic philosophy—is the art of being unseen in the work.

Sandy's aesthetic principle—her secret of artistic success—exists throughout every work she has created, and yet cannot be seen in any single work or its description. How is it possible to remain unseen in each piece and yet become visible when pieces are viewed in the aggregate? It is a matter of scale.

For the printer to remain unseen in an individual piece is an art in itself. Any technical imperfection is a give-away that the printer is still present, and removing imperfections is the first order of purifying a piece of the printer's presence. This accounts for Sandy's great attention to detail and to the demand that every copy of every piece be technically perfect. The archives of her project notebooks in the Special Collections of the Multnomah County Library in Portland are testimony to her concentration on the smallest of details, all designed to satisfy her exacting eye and thereby to avoid catching the eye of the reader. The ink, the paper, the choice of typeface and the arrangement and spacing of lines of type, the image, the collaboration with author and artist—all are the means Sandy has used to focus attention on the work itself. She continually experiments with new printing and imaging techniques in her work. But her technical standards and aesthetic philosophy remain the same. With intent she remains unseen in her individual work despite constant innovation and creativity. As one of her shows was aptly titled, "It's not about me."

The artistry of Sandy's work is a marvel when viewed in its entirety. Her technical excellence has been present from the start of her life as a fine press artist, whether the work is a binding, a broadside, or a book. Her aesthetic sensibilities emerged almost full-blown early in her vocation. Her art is literally a calling that she wants to be—has to be—an unseen agent for the spread and appreciation of the written word. As a result of this early call and fast-blossoming talent for design and printing excellence, it is difficult if not impossible to compare one of Sandy's pieces to another and tell which was done before the other, or at what point during the past twenty-seven years either was created. Since her graduation from the University of Alabama Book Arts program under the mentorship of Richard-Gabriel Rummonds, Sandy's work seems ahistorical, her early work as desirable for the collector to own as her most recent. She has no "Blue Period," no "Helvetica Period," no "University of Oregon Period." No periods, period.

Though Sandy's personal life is not seen in her work, neither is it absent. It is no accident that her immaculately maintained and arranged studio is filled with windows that not only provide abundant light but also create an ambience of openness to the larger world beyond printing. Her dogs, her garden, her home with Patrick all reflect a serene, natural continuity that informs her of who she is and why her art can speak for itself.

If the items selected for description in this book are taken in isolation, we lose in translation the grander nature of Sandy Tilcock's fine press printing. At the piece-level of analysis, we are looking at grains of sand and finding each unique, but never discovering on a larger scale that the grains constitute a beautiful beach. The beach is an abstraction of the same philosophy at the granular level—it frames, without necessarily delineating, an ocean of ideas expressed in wondrous words and images.

This book is intended, in part, to show how Sandy has channeled her artistic philosophy into unique, flawlessly crafted works of fine press printing that keep her larger goals as an artist unseen at the granular level. It is also intended to suggest, if not prove, that the whole of her work is much greater than the sum of the pieces. Each one of Sandy's works reveals an important aspect of her artistic philosophy, making it not only worthy of being acquired and preserved by collectors, but also worthy of being studied by future generations of printers.

— DENNIS HYATT

KLP18 **My Name Is Jane Grant (1999)**

Jane Grant

9.5 x 7 inches, single sheet

Handset Perpetua types

Cream Somerset Book paper

Letter of January 17, 1948, by Jane Grant

This keepsake was printed in celebration of the University of Oregon Library's exhibit "The Talk of the Town: Jane Grant, 'The New Yorker,' and the Oregon Legacy of a Twentieth Century Feminist".

KLP19 **After the Bach Festival (1999)**

W. Patrick Tilcock

11.5 x 6 inches, single sheet

Open edition

Handset Perpetua types

Cream Zerkall Book paper

KLP20 **Make Progress Every Day (2000)**

George Shipman

Image on page 90

4.2 x 2.6 inches

Handset Perpetua types

Somerset Book paper

Case covered in purple mohair book cloth with printed folio attached at the foredges using a hinge; red circle with Knight Library Press mark on front

This keepsake was presented to the staff of the University of Oregon Library upon the retirement of George W. Shipman, University Librarian, July 1980–June 2000.

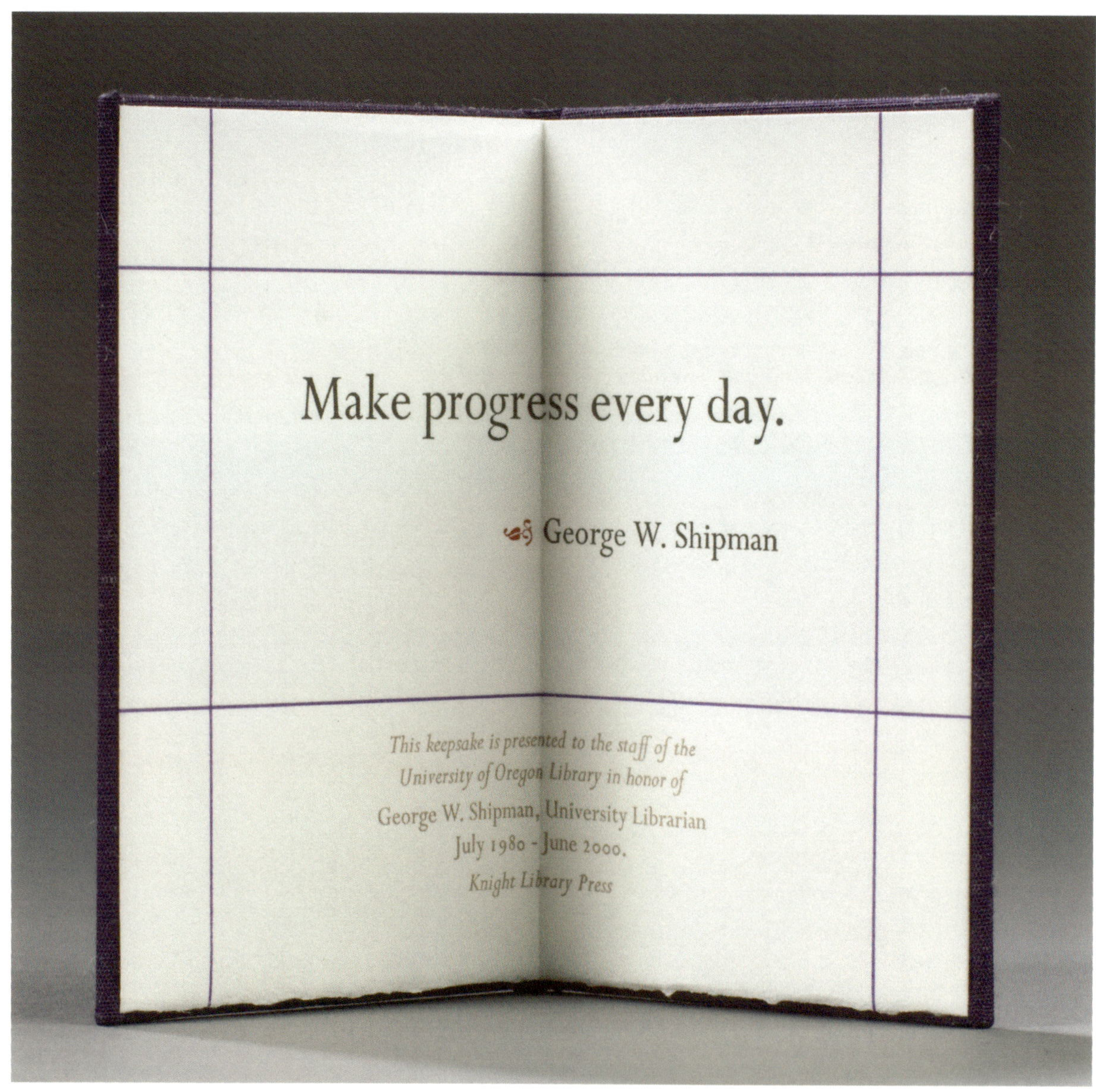
Make progress every day.
George W. Shipman
This keepsake is presented to the staff of the
University of Oregon Library in honor of
George W. Shipman, University Librarian
July 1980 - June 2000.
Knight Library Press

KLP20

KLP21 **Two on Two (2002)**

Brian Doyle
Original enso drawing by Marilyn Reaves reproduced using a polymer plate
Image on page 93

8.8 x 5.3 inches, 6 pages

150 numbered copies signed by the author

Handset Perpetua types; computer-set Castellar type for titling and initial and printed using photopolymer plates

Somerset Book paper

Accordion fold and sewn between the first and second panels to a paper cover of Canson Mi-Teintes

First published in *Creative Nonfiction* (Issue 9, 1998)

KLP22 **The Ultimate Mountain (2003)**

Ralph Salisbury
Drawing by Judith Sparks reproduced using a polymer plate
Image on page 92

8.5 x 5.375 inches, 4-page accordion fold

50 unsigned copies

Handset Centaur types

Somerset Velvet paper

Bound in boards with Thai Unryu paper and an image of Empress tree pods on front and back

KLP23 **Friend: Download This Free Proclamation for Local Use (2004)**

Kim Stafford

7.5 x 5 inches, single sheet broadside

500 copies

Handset Perpetua types

Mulberry paper

Designed to simulate a prayer flag, this single sheet is folded and pasted at top edge to hold a string hanger

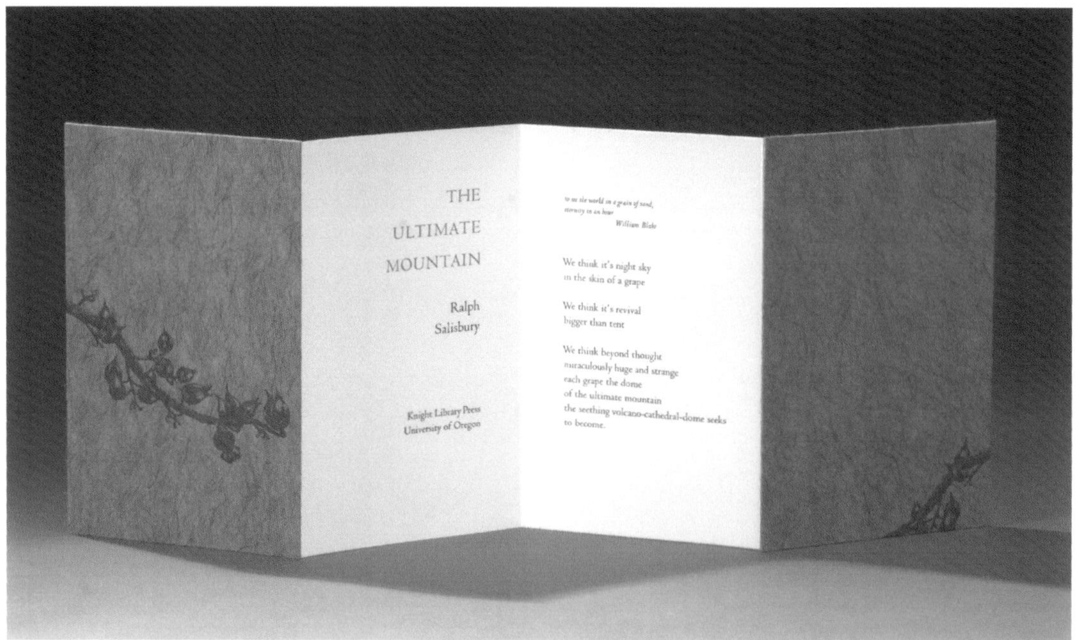

KLP22

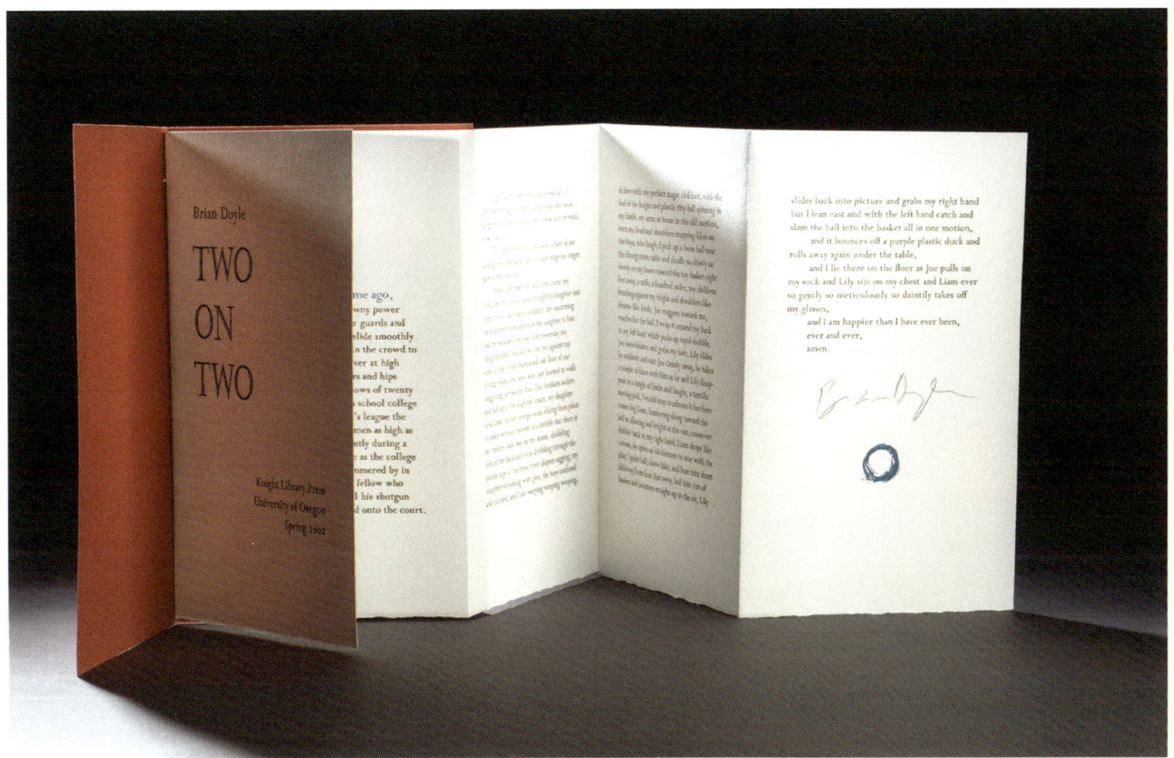
Brian Doyle
TWO
ON
TWO
Knight Library Press
University of Oregon
Spring 2002
slides back into picture and grabs my right hand
but I lean east and with the left hand catch and
slam the ball into the basket all in one motion,
and it bounces off a purple plastic duck and
rolls away again under the table,
and I lie there on the floor as Joe pulls on
my sock and Lily sits on my chest and Liam ever
so gently so meticulously so daintily takes off
my glasses,
and I am happier than I have ever been,
ever and ever,
amen.

KLP21

CONTRIBUTORS

Sandy Tilcock has been actively involved in book arts since her first calligraphy class in the fall of 1975. That passion grew and led her to establish lone goose press in the fall of 1989. Sandy likes to make things and loves the power of the printed word.

Patrick Tilcock has supported Sandy's creative explorations from the start of their journey together. A mental health worker and musician, he sometimes ventures into the precarious realm of writing poems.

Gabriel Rummonds operated the Plain Wrapper Press in Verona, Italy from 1971 until he moved it to Alabama in 1982 where he had been appointed to the faculty of the School of Library Sciences at the University of Alabama. Subsequently he was appointed director of the Book Arts Program. Mr. Rummonds is considered one of the leading hand press printers of the 20th century. While he no longer prints, he actively follows the careers of his students and continues to write about printing techniques. Gabriel's and Sandy's friendship has continued over the years since her graduation in 1987 and he always reviews her work with the critical eye of the mentor.

Barry Lopez is an author, essayist and short-story writer, and has traveled extensively in remote and sparsely populated parts of the world. He has received numerous honors and awards including the National Book Award for *Arctic Dreams*. In his nonfiction, Mr. Lopez writes often about the relationship between the physical landscape and human culture. In his fiction, he frequently addresses issues of intimacy, ethics, and identity. Barry has collaborated on limited editions with several presses including lone goose press and Knight Library Press.

Margot Voorhies Thompson is a painter, printmaker, designer and calligrapher who creates studio work as well as public art projects. Margot and Sandy have a long history dating back to Sandy's early work as a calligrapher. As a collaborator, Margot brings a wide repertoire of techniques and a willing, adventurous spirit.

Jim Carmin is the John Wilson Special Collections Librarian at Multnomah County Library in Portland, Oregon. Jim served on the Advisory Board of Knight Library Press during its tenure and it was at this time that a friendship developed between Sandy and Jim. It is because of his desire to use the lone goose press archives as a teaching tool that Sandy chose to house them in the John Wilson Special Collections.

Rennard Strickland is a legal historian of Indian law and is considered a pioneer in introducing Indian law into university curriculum. He was the dean of the University of Oregon School of Law when Sandy joined the University of Oregon as founding director of Knight Library Press. Rennard jumped at the chance to support the Press by commissioning its first major publication, *Far Off Shores*, which commemorated the opening of William W. Knight Law Center. Rennard commissioned several publications from both Knight Library Press and lone goose press. He loved the feel of paper, the smell of ink and the process in printing and binding a book by hand. Although he had a long publishing career, the fine press book / broadside allowed him to think of his writing in a new way and see new possibilities. He never sold his commissioned works, but delighted in giving them to friends and colleagues. Rennard encouraged Sandy to escape the confines of common expectations and dream of what could be.

Dennis Hyatt, a University of Oregon professor emeritus, was director of the University Law School Library from 1976–2004. Dennis began collecting Sandy's work in 1995 and subsequently became a subscriber. He took Sandy's Introduction to Fine Press Printing at the University of Oregon in 2000. It was here that he learned the challenges of the technical skills involved, Sandy's ideas on art and aspects of her creative process. Dennis continues to support Sandy's creative process to this day.

WORK COLLECTED BY THE FOLLOWING INSTITUTIONS

Arizona State University Libraries, Tempe, Arizona

The Heard Museum Library, Phoenix, Arizona

University of Arizona Library, Tucson, Arizona

Bancroft Library, University of California, Special Collections Library, Berkeley, California

Claremont Colleges Library, Claremont, California

Mills College, Special Collections Library, Oakland, California

Occidental College, Mary Norton Clapp Library, Los Angeles, California

Pepperdine University, Payson Library, Malibu, California

Scripps College, Denison Library, Claremont, California

Sonoma State University, Schulz Library, Rohnert Park, California

Stanford University, Special Collections Library, Palo Alto, California

University of California, Berkeley, Library, Berkeley, California

University of California, Davis, Shields Library, Davis, California

University of California, Irvine, Langson Library, Irvine, California

University of California, San Diego, UCSD Libraries, La Jolla, California

University of California, Santa Barbara, Davidson Library, Santa Barbara, California

University of Southern California, Doheny Library, Los Angeles, California

University of San Francisco, Gleeson Library, San Francisco, California

Colorado College, Tutt Library, Colorado Springs, Colorado

Denver Public Library, Special Collections, Denver, Colorado

University of Colorado at Boulder Library, Boulder, Colorado

University of Denver Libraries, Denver, Colorado

Yale University, Sterling Memorial Library, New Haven, Connecticut

University of Delaware, Hugh M. Morris Library, Newark, Delaware

Library of Congress, Washington, D.C.

Florida Atlantic University, Boca Raton Campus, S. E. Wimberly Library, Boca Raton, Florida

University of Georgia, Special Collections Library, Athens, Georgia

Boise State University, Albertsons Library, Boise, Idaho

Indiana University Library, Bloomington, Indiana

University of Iowa Libraries, Iowa City, Iowa

Topeka & Shawnee County Public Library, Topeka, Kansas

University of Kansas, Kenneth Spencer Research Library, Lawrence, Kansas

Louisiana State University, LSU Libraries, Baton Rouge, Louisiana

University of Louisiana at Lafayette, Edith Garland Dupre Library, Lafayette, Louisiana

Library of the Boston Athenaeum, Boston, Massachusetts

Smith College, Neilson Library, Northampton, Massachusetts

Wellesley College Library, Wellesley, Massachusetts

University of Minnesota Library, Minneapolis, Minnesota

University of Nevada, Reno, Mathewson-IGT Knowledge Center, Reno, Nevada

Dartmouth College Library, Hanover, New Hampshire

Princeton University Library, Princeton, New Jersey

New York Public Library, Special Collections Library, New York, New York

Rochester Institute of Technology, Wallace Library, Rochester, New York

State University of New York at Buffalo Library, Buffalo, New York

Union College, Schaffer Library, Schenectady, New York

Wells College, Wells Book Arts Center, Aurora, New York

Whitney Museum Library, Special Collections Library, New York, New York

Duke University Library, Durham, North Carolina

Mint Museum of Arts & Crafts, Charlotte, North Carolina

University of North Carolina at Greensboro Libraries, Greensboro, North Carolina

University of Oklahoma, Law Center Library, Norman, Oklahoma

Lewis & Clark College, Aubrey R. Watzek Library, Portland, Oregon

Multnomah County Library, John Wilson Special Collections, Portland, Oregon

Portland Art Museum Archive, Portland, Oregon

Reed College Library, Portland, Oregon

University of Oregon, Special Collections Library, Eugene, Oregon

University of Portland, Wilson W. Clark Memorial Library, Portland Oregon

Lafayette College Library, Easton, Pennsylvania

Brown University, John Hay Library, Providence, Rhode Island

Texas Christian University Library, Fort Worth, Texas

Texas Tech University, Southwest Collection, Lubbock, Texas

University of Texas at Austin, Harry Ransom Humanities Research Center, Austin, Texas

Brigham Young University, Harold B. Lee Library, Provo, Utah

University of Utah, J. Willard Marriott Library, Salt Lake City, Utah

Utah State University, Merrill-Cazier Library, Logan, Utah

Middlebury College Library, Middlebury, Vermont

University of Vermont, Bailey/Howe Library, Burlington, Vermont

George Mason University, Fenwick Library, Fairfax, Virginia

Seattle University, Lemieux Library and McGoldrick Learning Commons, Seattle, Washington

University of Puget Sound, Collins Memorial Library, Tacoma, Washington

University of Washington Libraries, Seattle, Washington

Washington State Library, Tumwater, Washington

Washington State University, Holland and Terrell Libraries, Pullman, Washington

Wisconsin Historical Society, Madison, Wisconsin

Brandon University, John E. Robbins Library, Brandon, Manitoba, Canada

Hong Kong Baptist University, HBKU Library, Kowloon, Hong Kong

The British Library, St. Pancras American Collections, London, United Kingdom

Typefaces:

Text—Gill Sans
Display—Beata

Photo credits:

Front cover—George Filgate
Back cover—Petar Iliev
Weathergram on page 45—Sandy Tilcock
Last page (Sandy at the press)—A. J. Adams
All other photos—Jon Christopher Meyers

Designers:

Dune Erickson
Sandy Tilcock

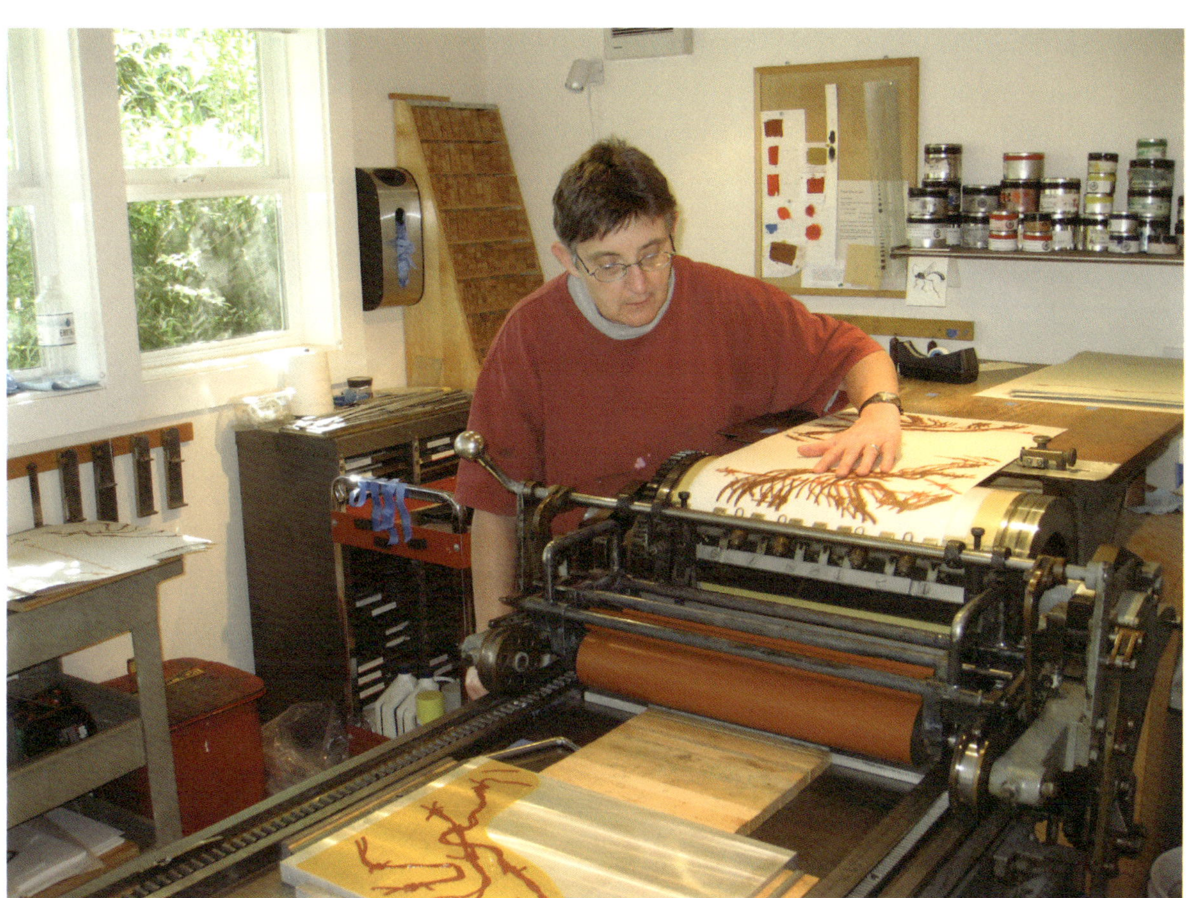

CPSIA information can be obtained at www.ICGtesting.com
Printed in the USA
BVIW12n0639271216
471706BV00023B/32